The Reference Shelf

Terrorism in the United States

Edited by Frank McGuckin

The Reference Shelf
Volume 69 • Number 1

The H. W. Wilson Company
New York • Dublin
1997

Reference Shelf

rints of articles, excerpts from books, and addresses n the United States and other countries. There are six volume, all of which are generally published in the same calendar year. Numbers one through five are each devoted to a single subject, providing background information and discussion from various points of view and concluding with a comprehensive bibliography that lists books, pamphlets and abstracts of additional articles on the subject. The final number of each volume is a collection of recent speeches. This number also contains a subject index to all the articles in an entire Reference Shelf volume. Books in the series may be purchased individually or on subscription.

Visit H.W. Wilson's web site: http://www.hwwilson.com

Library of Congress Cataloging-in-Publication Data

Terrorism in the United States / edited by Frank McGuckin.
    p.   cm. — (The reference shelf ; v. 69, no. 1)
    Includes bibliographical references and index.
    ISBN 0-8242-0914-1
    1. Terrorism—United States. 2. United States—Social conditions—1980-.
3. United States—Political and government—1989-.
I. McGuckin, Frank, 1971- . II. Series.
HV6432.T45 1997
303.6'25'0973—dc21   97-3423
                                                                        CIP

Cover: A state of emergency at the federal building in Oklahoma City, which was
        bombed April 19, 1995.

Photo: AP/Wide World Photos

Printed in the United States of America

Contents

5

Preface

While terrorist actions are not new to American soil, they have not, until recently, been a common occurrence inside America's borders. Consequently, American experience with terrorist activity has been typically restricted to the reading of an exclamatory newspaper headline, or the viewing of film footage taken in a distant nation. Examples include the 1983 suicide bombing of a U.S. base in Beirut, which killed 241 Marines, and the 1988 bombing of Pan Am flight 103 over Lockerbie, Scotland, in which 270 perished. Even though hundreds of Americans died in these incidents, terrorism remained in the arena of international affairs and was not seen as a part of the national landscape.

In 1993, Islamic extremists detonated a bomb deep inside New York City's World Trade Center, killing six and injuring hundreds. *The New Republic* described the explosion as "an occasion to recognize that...violent habits...are gradually slipping across our borders." The blast on April 19, 1995, that gutted the federal building in Oklahoma City, killed over 160 people and injured hundreds of others, suggests that these lethal "habits" are not only making their way into America, but are practiced by Americans themselves. Although the Oklahoma City bombing was at first thought to be the work of foreign extremists, the su pects now on trial are native-born Americans with ties to home-grown militia groups seems fair to say that terrorism is no longer a distant and foreign affair but also a domestic problem; the explosions and gun-fire are no longer experienced at second through the media, but directly in the daily lives of an increasing number of citi

As terrorism becomes more prevalent within America's borders, our interest i es, methods, and effects substantially grows. Sensationalism and emotion a ism remains, as Webster initially defined it, a "means of coercion...through ic use [and creation] of terror." It is therefore neither blind nor random rather an action devoted and targeted toward the realization of a goal. tematic," premeditated, and calculated, and the resulting death-and-inj be U.S. Marines (as in Beirut), or children (as in Oklahoma), is not i Such carnage is simply a means to an end, part of the larger envi fear which the terrorist wishes to create in order to undermine e gain a hearing for his or her specific cause.

This volume opens with a series of articles on the political the terrorist mindset. Tracing the similarities which exist be regardless of political affiliation, Section I, "The Cultu describes the terrorist as a person who believes that h absolute value and are under threat from the existing relates the violent cultural climate within our nation terrorism, suggesting that terrorists are not bizarre resentative of the culture in which they occur.

Section II, "The Terrorist and the Terrorist A cussion to a sampling of the actual groups, linked to terrorist violence—a surprising defenders of liberty to Islamist opponents

erally share is a deeply adversarial attitude toward the federal government and a conviction that violence for a cause may at times be justified, even desirable. Some of these "fringe" groups exhibit formidable levels of organization, intelligence, and skill, to say nothing of funding. But whether they have gone beyond passionate rhetoric to engage in violent action is unclear, and a dilemma for law enforcement.

Aside from the immediate bloodshed, a terrorist event also prompts investigations, political rhetoric, and changes in the way we live. Section III, "The Effects of Terrorism," provides a sampling of the occurrences that follow a terrorist event. Containing quotes from politicians, first-hand accounts of familial devastation, and complaints about the inquisition-like nature of a federal investigation, this section conveys the ripple effect that occurs after a terrorist event and the multitude of people who are ultimately affected by it.

The last section, entitled "Preventive Measures," discusses various proposals for preventing terrorism. The prevention of terrorism is neither simple nor clear-cut. It may involve encroachments upon civil liberties, and so it forces us to question the point at which security measures become overly restrictive and intrusive.

The articles in this volume of Reference Shelf have been collected to portray the increasing number of American groups and coalitions willing to resort to violent action; to probe the mindset, aims, politics, and methods of the terrorist; and to describe both the immediate and long-term effects of a terrorist event. To forestall such events, we must recognize not only the threat of terrorism and the increasing complexities of that threat, but also the fundamental discontent that is represented by the terrorist action.

The editor would like to thank the authors and publishers who have granted permission to reprint their material in this compilation.

Frank McGuckin
January 1997

I. The Culture and Politics of Terrorism

Editor's Introduction

Composed of articles which discuss terrorist ideology and psychology, Section I attempts to answer the questions: What are the historical/political roots of terrorism?; Why is violence becoming a more common course of action?; How is American culture consciously or unconsciously accommodating increased terrorism?; and How are individual terrorists linked together, in terms of their similar motivations and mindsets? As important as it is to understand the specific nature of a given terrorist, it is equally important to understand the less tangible background factors through cultural and political analysis. In many cases, as these articles will reveal, the primary motivation for a terrorist is a genuine frustration with seemingly intractable political, social, and economic forces.

The first article of Section I, "America's Bomb Culture," by Christopher John Farley, writing in *Time* magazine, analyzes the FBI's Bomb Data Center statistics to establish a correlation between the "dissemination of bomb know-how" and the rising incidence of actual bombings. In the process, Farley portrays a culture that is all too accommodating to the violence inherent to terrorist activity. The second article, "Connect the Dots," by Frank Rich of *The New York Times*, examines the political ideologies of extremist militia groups. Just as Farley, in the first article of this section, strives to link terrorist action with mainstream culture, Rich searches out links between groups with apparently disparate agendas—opponents of gun control, anti-abortion extremists, Christian fundamentalists, white supremacists, and a range of paramilitary militias. At the very least, Rich demonstrates how thin a line can separate gross political and social discontent from a terrorist's rationale.

In a speech given by David B. Kopel, entitled "The Federal Government Should Set a Better Example," the increase of federal authority and the perceived violence of federal law enforcement are cited as contributing to the increase in domestic terrorism. Kopel asserts that the best way to defuse the growing American militia movement is to curb the federal government's power and avoid the abusive behavior that characterized the assault on the Branch-Davidian compound at Waco, Texas, and the siege of Ruby Ridge in Idaho.

Tom Bethell, writing in *The American Spectator*, calls the recent growth in terrorism primarily a reaction to a "federal government [that] has accumulated too much power, and needs to back off." In the article entitled "Turnabout Is Fair Play," Bethel, arguing in a conservative vein, decries the growth in federal power that has occurred in recent years and theorizes that the increase in national terrorism is related to the post–World War II expansion of federal authority and the consequent reduction of state power.

Through a historical treatise on liberty and violence which includes excerpts from political thinkers such as Edmund Burke and John Stuart Mill, Conor Cruise O'Brien separates revolutionary terrorism from "ordered liberty." O'Brien, writing in *National Review*, remarks that both liberalism and terrorism share a devotion to freedom. The difference lies in the fact that terrorism is "absolutist and unappeasable," not open to compromise or concession. O'Brien is pessimistic about the ability of Western liberals to meet the challenge posed by terrorist campaigns.

America's Bomb Culture[1]

Some New Jersey teenagers fax two bomb threats to their high school in an alleged attempt to extort $1.3 million. In the home of one of them, police find a bombmaking manual called *Jolly Roger's Cookbook*, which, they say, had been downloaded from the Internet. In Albuquerque, New Mexico, a live grenade is found in a newspaper-vending box; a day later, police discover an 8-in. pipe bomb on a bridge. These incidents, which happened last week and caused no injury, may seem almost mundane compared to tragedy on the scale of the Oklahoma City blast and the notoriety of the Unabomber. Yet they represent a far more insidious danger: America's growing fascination and familiarity with bombs. In real life and in the movies, exploding devices have become common-place. Joseph Grubisic, the commander of the Chicago police department's bomb squad, has seen an increase in bomb use by Cook County gangs and drug rings. His unit coined the term MacGyver bombs to identify a class of homemade devices he believes were inspired by the TV series. "We get a dozen or so a year," he says.

"In 1993, bombs killed 43 and injured 281, up from 29 dead and 230 wounded two years earlier."

Grubisic's experience is reflected in the data collected by the FBI's Bomb Data Center, which counted 1,880 bombings in 1993, up from 442 a decade earlier. In 1993, bombs killed 43 and injured 281, up from 29 dead and 230 wounded two years earlier. The increase does not take into account the six deaths and 1,042 injuries caused by the 1993 bombing of the World Trade Center. According to the Bureau of Alcohol, Tobacco and Firearms, about half the bombing attempts in 1993 were acts of vandalism, 13% were intended as revenge and fewer than 1% were acts of protest.

A significant factor in the increase in bombings is that the dissemination of bomb know-how has become a minor industry. The past few decades have produced the rise of mail-order publishing companies that serve the so-called gun aftermarket, including the gun fanciers, survivalists, wannabe cops and closet anarchists who like to shop for such products as laser sights, camouflage, fake badges and fake FBI and ATF hats. Some of their most popular offerings are "burn-and-blow" books that describe in detail how to make landmines, booby traps and bombs. "The information is available on the Internet and everywhere else," says retired ATF agent Al Gleason, who spent 50 years investigating bombings. "People who feel that the bomb might be their weapon of choice now have the information to make one."

One of the earliest and most successful products of these publishers is the *Anarchist Cookbook*, which was put out in 1971 by Lyle Stuart Inc. But to bomb-squad commanders, the most notori-

---

[1]Article by Christopher John Farley, from *Time*, 145:56 My 8, '95. Copyright © 1995 TIME INC. Reprinted with permission.

ous publisher is Paladin Press in Boulder, Colorado, founded in 1970 by two Special Forces veterans of the Vietnam War. The company carries a catalog of 40 books and videos on how to make explosives, including the *Improvised Munitions Black Book* series-repackaged versions of military manuals with instructions for building explosives. Paladin's list also carries *Homemade C-4: A Recipe for Survival*, about which one catalog edition says, "Serious survivors know that the day may come when they need something more powerful than commercial dynamite...For blowing bridges, shattering steel and derailing tanks, they need C-4."

Burn-and-blow publishers argue that there is no correlation between their material, which often carries the caveat "for information purposes only," and the increasing rate of bombings across the nation. "I sell a thousand books, but there ain't a thousand explosions," says Billy Blann, the owner of Delta Press Ltd. of El Dorado, Arkansas. The flurry of orders after the Oklahoma bombing for the pamphlet *Improvised Munitions from Ammonium Nitrate*, he says, is "just armchair people who want to know what's going on."

Hollywood too has become fascinated. With gunplay so common in real life, producers have turned to bombers as the villains du jour. On TV, the season finale of *Melrose Place* features a character who sets off a bomb at the apartment complex that houses the show's cast. The ABC soap opera *All My Children* contains a story line in which a character has been planning to bomb an ex-lover on his wedding day. In the wake of the Oklahoma bombing, producers of the soap opera say they are altering the bomb angle, while *Melrose Place*'s producers are considering the same measure. At the movies, the new Chuck Norris film *Top Dog* begins with the bombing of an apartment building by neo-Nazis. Due May 19 is the Bruce Willis thriller *Die Hard with a Vengeance*, which opens with the

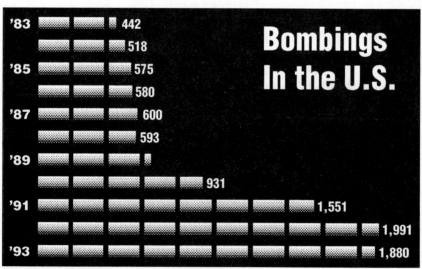

'83 442
518
'85 575
580
'87 600
593
'89
931
'91 1,551
1,991
'93 1,880

Bombings In the U.S.

Source: FBI Bomb Data Center

bombing of a department store. Bombings have been featured in
Speed, *Blown Away* and *The Specialist*. Moviemakers contend that
they are merely reflecting reality. Says Graham Yost, the screen-
writer for *Speed*: "We looked at bombings taking place all around
the world and basically brought the conflict home to America."
Tragically, real-life bombers maybe doing the same thing.

Connect the Dots[2]

When the full history of home-grown American terrorism in the 1990's is written, the chapter before Oklahoma City will tell of a little-noticed press conference last August in New York.

It was called by Planned Parenthood to showcase a videotape of a meeting held by the Wisconsin branch of the far-right U.S. Taxpayers Party. The meeting's speakers included two of the country's most militant anti-abortion leaders, Randall Terry of Operation Rescue and Matthew Trewhella of Missionaries to the Preborn. But they weren't talking about abortion. Mr. Trewhella spoke of training his young child to use guns. The meeting's attendees were offered a manual titled "Principles Justifying the Arming and Organizing of a Militia" in which the Bible was invoked to justify the formation of "assault teams" to protect the unborn.

For Planned Parenthood, which had been forced by Reagan-era Federal indifference to do its own research into the steep 1980's rise in abortion-clinic bombings and murder, this demonstrable link between anti-abortion extremists and a growing militia movement was a major breakthrough. In the stepped-up investigation that followed, Planned Parenthood began to uncover a commingling of anti-abortion extremists, new-world-order paranoids, Waco wackos, Reconstructionist Christians, white supremacists and assault-weapon fanatics in a national paramilitary subculture. Abortion turned out to be merely the come-on issue, designed to attract followers to a rabid anti-government crusade.

Since the Oklahoma bombing, Federal law enforcement officials have been in constant touch with Planned Parenthood, explained Pamela Maraldo, the organization's president. By now they've no doubt seen an anti-abortion terrorism manual from the mid-1980's with an elaborate illustrated plan for building a fertilizer bomb. Presumably the F.B.I. is also consulting the Southern Poverty Law Center, the Anti-Defamation League and the American Jewish Committee, which, like Planned Parenthood, were driven by criminality in their own backyards to investigate the paramilitary right. As the Jewish weekly *The Forward* reported last week, anti-Semitic violence in the militia strongholds of Idaho and Montana is now routine.

It's not yet known whether this evidence will connect a specific militia or far-right group to the Oklahoma tragedy. What is clear is how extensively the nation's far-right factions are interconnected, forming a political network that often publicly espouses the same ideology as the terrorists in our midst, much as the Sinn Fein speaks aboveground for the I.R.A.

For one example of the far right's cohesiveness, consider

[2]Article by Frank Rich, from *The New York Times* D15 Ap 30, '95. Copyright © 1995 The New York Times Company. Reprinted with permission.

Lawrence Pratt, head of the rabid Gun Owners of America. Wearing another hat, Mr.Pratt also runs the Committee to Protect the Family Foundation, a fund-raiser for Operation Rescue. As a public speaker, Mr. Pratt tours with "Preparedness Expo '95," where he shares top billing with Mark ("from Michigan") Koernke, the shortwave radio voice of the militia movement, and Bo Gritz, the Idaho militia guru and Christian Covenant leader who last week described the Oklahoma bombing as "a Rembrandt—a masterpiece of science and art put together."

And who is the biggest recipient of campaign funds from Mr. Pratt's Gun Owners of America? None other than Representative Steve Stockman, the Texas Republican who last week denied any connection to militias when asked to explain the mysterious fax his office received after the Oklahoma bombing. Even so, *Roll Call*, the Capitol Hill paper, condemned Mr. Stockman and Idaho's Representative Helen Chenoweth on Thursday in an editorial titled "Paranoid Fringe."

At last, though at a high price, the country and Justice Department are starting to catch up to Planned Parenthood. As Frederick Clarkson, one of its researchers of the radical right, says: "Abortion clinics have had an average of 15 bombings or arsons every year for a decade. If that had happened at churches or newspapers or Federal office buildings, we would have called it terrorism. But society didn't want to recognize the pattern of violence."

Now that we're starting to recognize the complexity of that pattern,we also see that even when all the Oklahoma City bombing suspects arearrested, the investigation will have only just begun.

The Federal Government Should Set a Better Example[3]

Militias and Gun Control

From my own family background, people who threaten violence against government employees are particularly frightening. For most of my childhood, my father's twenty-two year career in the Colorado House of Representatives was in progress. When he chaired the House Judiciary Committee, he steered to House passage the only major gun control—a ban on so-called "Saturday Night Specials"—that has passed any house of the Colorado legislature in the last twenty-five years.

My mother served during the 1970s and 1980s as the Colorado and Kansas director of the federal government's United States bankruptcy trustee program. Before I went to work for a think tank, I served as an assistant attorney general for the Colorado Attorney General's Office, handling enforcement of environmental laws.

The cowardly criminals who killed so many innocent people in Oklahoma City could just as well have killed my mother, my father, or myself. Just as much as any other citizen of the United States, government employees are absolutely entitled to live their lives free of criminal violence and criminal intimidation.

It is wrong to dehumanize any class of people, and that includes people such as my family who work for the government. Persons who advocate and perpetrate criminal violence against government employees are no less wrongful as any other criminals who act out of prejudice and bigotry.

It is essential that government employees, like all other Americans, be safe. Not just physically safe, but safe to go about their lives free of fear, and free to exercise all of their civil and Constitutional rights.

As we think about safety, it is important not to fool ourselves. Far too often in America, legislatures, including Congress, having misunderstood or been misled about potential threats, and have enacted repressive legislation that has sacrificed liberty without improving safety.

In the United States, there is a long sad history of interest groups or government officials taking a few isolated incidents and inflating them into some kind of vast threat, requiring an immediate, repressive response. Back in 1798, President John Adams and the Federalists who controlled Congress were scandalized by the vicious campaigns against them in the press. These scurrilous charges—such as accusations that President Adams had sent

[3]Speech delivered by David B. Kopel, Associate Policy Analyst, Independent Institute, to the Subcommittee on Crime of the Committees on the Judiciary, U.S. House of Representatives, from *Vital Speeches of the Day* 62:315-19 Mr. 1, '96. Copyright © 1996 City News Publishing Co. Reprinted with permission.

General Pinckney to England to procure a pair of
for him—show that today's political mudslinging
is, is nothing new.

At the same time, in these turbulent years follc
revolution, the French government worked furi
American support in the French conflict with Engl
cials attempted to bribe American newspapers to
side in the conflict—and to criticize the pro-Eng
President Adams.

President Adams, unfortunately reacted in a mann
set a pattern of federal error. Because a few of his
nents were motivated by foreign bribes, he assumed
cal opponents as a whole were illegitimate. In 1798, Cc
ed and President Adams signed the Alien and Seditior

This hated Act allowed the extrajudicial deportation of legal resi-
dent aliens whom the Administration considered to be a security
threat. Criticism of the President was termed "sedition" and out-
lawed. Guilt by association was used to tar all Jeffersonians as dis-
loyal.

Rather than calming the political waters, the Alien and Sedition
Acts provoked a furious backlash. The Kentucky and Virginia
Resolutions were enacted, in which state legislatures asserted the
authority to nullify within their territory, laws which violated the
Constitution—as the Alien and Sedition Acts certainly did.

Had President Adams decided to force the issue, civil war might
have resulted. Happily, the Alien and Sedition Acts were never vigorously enforced. After Thomas Jefferson was elected in 1800, the
Acts were repealed.

Decades later, a violent, deranged abolitionist named John Brown
led a raid on the federal armory at Harper's Ferry, hoping to set off
a massive slave rebellion. John Brown's delusional scheme was
rapidly suppressed, and Brown was tried and executed. But John
Brown's isolated act combined with the extremist rhetoric of some
abolitionists led many Southern state legislatures to conclude that
all the critics of slavery were part of some fearsome conspiracy to
promote violent revolution and to destroy the South. Laws were
enacted which suppressed anti-slavery speech throughout the
South.

Abolitionists and slave owners both saw each other only in dis-
torted stereotypes. The polarization led, of course, to the tremendous suffering of the Civil War, and in the long run to a solution to
slavery which unfortunately, left many ex-slaves in a condition of
virtual slavery.

In the decades following the Civil War, the political leadership
again overreacted to organizations which challenged the existing
system. During much of the nineteenth century, and indeed a good
part of the twentieth, conspiracy laws were used against unions and
union organizers. Criminal syndicalism laws (an updated version of
John Adams' sedition laws) were employed against radical unions
such as the "Wobblies" (the International Workers of the World).

During that period, some labor leaders were indeed people who sought the violent overthrow of the government. Some of them harbored various conspiracy theories, including anti-Semitic ones. For decades, many states governments, and often the federal government, engaged in a policy of confrontation and war against this threat. Labor violence convulsed the nation. The year 1876—the centennial of the United States of America—was wracked by labor riots in one major city after another. The old armories that one can find in the downtown of almost every major American city that was a city during the late 19th century were often built for suppressing labor riots. The Haymarket Massacre was one of the bloodiest, but hardly the only, tragedy resulting from a confrontation between militarized law enforcement and groups which the political system deemed unacceptable.

"Especially in the 1950s, criticism of the free enterprise system or of militarism was falsely equated with disloyalty."

Some of the riot leaders were Communists or other advocates of violent overthrow. But a generally hostile press and political establishment overestimated the pervasiveness of such sentiments. Most workers simply wanted better working conditions, and a better share of the wealth that they helped produce.

In the end, it was the protection of the rights of working people, and negotiation over legitimate grievances, which led to an abatement of labor strife.

Even in the twentieth century, radical critiques of the government have too often been met with fierce government repression. During World War I, Eugene Debs's peaceful criticism of the draft landed him in federal prison.

During the Cold War, legitimate concerns about Soviet spies and their American accomplices (such as the Rosenbergs and Alger Hiss) led to repressive legislation, blacklists, loyalty oaths, and other infringements on the freedoms which distinguished America from the Soviet Union. Especially in the 1950s, criticism of the free enterprise system or of militarism was falsely equated with disloyalty.

At about the same time, many Southern state governments, as well as the F.B.I., were aware that "Communist agitators" were among those involved in the civil rights movement, as indeed they had been since at least the 1930s. But the presence of a few Communists within the civil rights movement or its leadership (like the earlier presence of Communists within the labor movement), did not mean the civil rights movement was fundamentally communist, or that it should be suppressed—although that is precisely what many state governments attempted to do for many years.

If it is easy for many Americans to see, in hindsight, the legitimacy of the viewpoint of Jeffersonians, of southern abolitionists, of labor organizers, of critics of militarism, and of the civil rights movement, it is not so easy for some Americans to respect the fundamental concerns of the many millions of their fellow citizens who are frightened of the federal government.

Today, there are many tens of millions of people who are frightened of the government, and many thousands (or perhaps more) who participate in militias. Some of them may have incorrect beliefs about the Brady Bill or the ban on so-called "assault weapons," or the United Nations, or other political issues. But allegedly mistaken beliefs are no basis for federal jurisdiction.

Within these groups, as there are within almost any other group, a few criminals. Just as citizens should not imagine that because a few Congress people are found guilty of felonies most Congress people are criminals, Congress people should not imagine that because a few persons with anti-government viewpoints are criminals, many or most militia members or other government critics are criminals.

Let us learn from history. Let us not be panicked into hasty action that history will judge harshly. Let us begin a process of respectful dialogue and reform, not stereotyping and repression.

As Justice Brandeis understood, "Repression breeds hate; hate menaces stable government; the path of safety lies in the opportunity to discuss freely supposed grievances and proposed remedies."

One of the reasons that so many people have become fearful of the federal government, and some have become angry, has been the virtually uninterrupted expansion of federal laws, at the expense of civil liberty. The cycle of misleading media sensationalism, a couple of Congressional hearings, and then another broad and intrusive federal "remedy" has become all too familiar.

"Let us begin a process of respectful dialogue and reform, not stereotyping and repression."

It is possible to assemble before any given Congressional panel a half-dozen very sincere witnesses who will claim that any given topic is 1. An immense problem; 2. Rapidly spiraling out of control all over the nation; and 3. Desperately in need of an immediate, sweeping federal remedy.

Sometimes these witnesses are correct. But other times they are not.

We know in retrospect that the Marihuana Tax Act of the 1930s was the result of a racist campaign of disinformation about the use of marijuana by Hispanic criminals. We know that the Food Stamp Act in the early 1970s was passed as a result of tremendous misinformation about the extent of malnutrition in rural America. We know that, despite the wild claims of various law enforcement administrators, so-called "assault weapons" constitute only about one percent of crime guns seized by police, even in major cities. A climate of panic and misinformation about the Love Canal incident in New York led Congress to enact the Superfund law—a draconian law which imposes huge retroactive liability on companies and individuals for lawful environmental practices, and which eliminates most ordinary due process protections for individuals targeted by the government.

Before enacting additional legislation in an atmosphere of media hype and prejudice, Congress would do well to slow down.

For example, we have no reliable hard data about how often government employees are being threatened or attacked. Still less do we have any hard data about how often existing state and federal laws are inadequate to punish the criminals involved.

Current criminal laws do not require that authorities wait until someone has actually been injured or killed. Making threats is, of course, a crime in itself.

Nor are states necessarily helpless or unwilling to act. In no state are the people who perpetrate or support violent crimes against government officials the majority of the population. Or even close to it.

Some problems are plainly inappropriate for a federal "solution." For example, some persons—living proof of the principle that a little knowledge is a dangerous thing—have begun filing purported liens or other alleged "common law," instruments in some state courts. Surely the remedy for abuse of state court procedures is through enforcement of existing procedural rules which punish frivolous or false legal filings, or through reforms of state court systems to provide whatever additional remedies may be needed. State courts are the business of the states, not of Congress.

"...the federal racketeering statute (RICO) was enacted in the 1970s,...it would provide an important new weapon to target organized crime organizations..."

The spirit of the Tenth Amendment suggests that before federal legislature acts, it considers what the state legislatures, and the people of the states decide to do. For example, one group in Montana is planning a ballot initiative to strengthen states laws against threatening government officials. Perhaps the law will be carefully tailored to address local conditions in Montana. Or perhaps the people of Montana will choose a different approach. But in any case, it ought to be the people of Montana, not 535 people—of whom only three are from Montana—who decide what to do.

When the federal racketeering statute (RICO) was enacted in the 1970s, proponents promised that it would provide an important new weapon to target organized crime organizations, as opposed to prosecuting only individual criminals.

But RICO statute has also been used in ways which its sponsors never foresaw. For example, in the 1980s, an ambitious United States Attorney in New York City used RICO's pre-emptive strike provisions to destroy a securities firm, First Princeton, which was, years later, found to be guilty of absolutely no wrongdoing. But in the meantime, the company had been mined, the employees had lost their jobs, and the owners had lost their business and the assets which they had built over years through honest hard work.

In other cases, RICO laws have been used against abortion clinic protesters. Instead of using Mafia laws against church groups, it would be better to fashion—as many legislatures have—more specific statutes which deal with the particular problem of access to abortion clinics.

In regards to anti-government violence, proposals for broad new conspiracy statutes, or for broad new judicial authority to destroy or disband organizations have not been shown to be necessary—particularly at a federal level.

We know from history that injunction and conspiracy laws have often been used unfairly against political dissidents, such as labor organizers.

Moreover, the criminally violent anti-government organizations which are the focus of today's hearing are, almost without exception, tiny. Prosecution of the handful of criminal individuals involved will suffice to destroy the pathetic "organization" itself.

New federal mandatory minimums seem, sadly, to be instinctive reaction of some persons to almost every human ill. Mandatory minimums, by their nature, prevent judges and prosecutors from tailoring the punishment to the facts of the particular case, and as a result, injustice too often results. Some of the new proposed mandatory minimums for "violent anti-government extremists" would impose a two-year mandatory minimum on someone who shoved a policeman during an argument over a traffic ticket, a two-year mandatory minimum on a jilted teenage girl who sent her rival an anonymous letter "I'm going to tear your eyes out," and an eight year mandatory minimum on a homeowner who waved a baseball bat at a zoning inspector. None of these activities are justified, of course, and none of them are the intended target of the proposed mandatory minimums. But mandatory minimums are perversely designed to apply remedies which seem appropriate in the abstract to situations where they may be wildly inappropriate.

Oddly, today's hearings about "Violent Anti-Government Groups" and the threat they pose to local governments may be used to promote legislation aimed squarely at constricting, not helping, local governments. According to section 7 of the draft "Republican Form of Government Guarantee Act," when county governments enforce state and local laws against what they believe to be illegal conduct by federal employees, the federal government will become the judge of its own case. Rather than having the dispute settled by a neutral arbiter—the courts—the dispute will be investigated by the federal employees own chief lawyer (the Attorney General), who may then unilaterally withhold Payments in Lieu of Taxes from the county.

It is an elementary principle of justice that no person (nor the person's attorney) can be the judge of his own case. And it's a misuse of language to claim that the federal executive's judging its own case in disputes with counties will somehow further the federal government's obligation to guarantee to each state a republican form of government. County commissioners are, after all, democratically elected. They—not the federal executive branch—are part of a state's republican form of government. Equating all militias with white supremacists is nonsense. Like the Los Angeles Police Department, some militias may have members, or even officers, who are racist, but that does not mean that the organization as a whole, or the vast majority of its members are racists. Most militias are composed of people with jobs and families; people who are seeking to protect what they have, not to inflict revenge on others for their own failings.

The frenzy of hatred being whipped up against law-abiding militia members is not unlike the hatred to which law-abiding Arab-Americans would have been subjected, had Oklahoma City been perpetrated by the Libyan secret service. It is not unlike the hatred to which Japanese-Americans were subjected after World

War II. Ironically, some politicians who complain about the coarse, angry tone of American politics do so in speeches in which they heap hate-filled invective upon anyone and everyone who belongs to a militia.

As this testimony is written, no evidence has developed which ties any militia (let alone all of them) to the Oklahoma City crime. At most, two suspects are said to have attended a few militia meetings and left because the militias did not share their goals. This fact no more proves a militia conspiracy than the hypothetical fact that the suspects went to church a few times would prove that the Pope and Jerry Falwell masterminded the Oklahoma City bombings.

That someone who perpetrated a crime may have attended a militia meeting is hardly proof that all militias should be destroyed. The step-father of Susan Smith (the South Carolina child murderer) sexually molested her one night after he returned from putting up posters for the Pat Robertson presidential campaign. What if someone suggested that the "radical" patriarchal theories espoused by Robertson and the Christian Coalition created the "atmosphere" which led to the incestuous rape, and that therefore all Christian Coalition members were responsible for the crime, and the FBI should "crack down" on them? The claim would be dismissed in a second; equally outrageous claims about gun owners should likewise be dismissed.

It is a sad testament to the bigotry of certain segments of the media that totally unsubstantiated, vicious conspiracy theories of the type which were once employed against Catholics and Jews are now being trotted out against militia members, patriots, and gun owners.

No militia group was involved with the Oklahoma City bombing. Despite the hate-mongering of the media, the "need" to start spying on militia groups is a totally implausible basis for expansion of federal government powers.

To respond intelligently to the militia and patriot movements, we must acknowledge that, although the movements are permeated with implausible conspiracy theories, the movements are a reaction to increasing militarization, lawlessness, and violence of federal law enforcement, a genuine problem which should concern all Americans.

We must also remember that it is lawful in the United States to exercise freedom of speech and the right to bear arms. Spending one's weekends in the woods practicing with firearms and listening to right-wing political speeches is not my idea of a good time, but there is not, and should not, be anything illegal about it.

If we want to shrink the militia movement, the surest way is to reduce criminal and abusive behavior by the federal government, and to require a thorough, open investigation by a Special Prosecutor of what happened at Waco and at Ruby Ridge, Idaho. If, as the evidence strongly suggests, the law was broken, the law-breakers should be prosecuted, even if they happen to be government employees.

Conversely, the persons responsible for the deaths of innocent Americans should not be promoted to even-higher positions in the FBI or federal law enforcement. If the Clinton administration were trying to fan the flames of paranoia, it could hardly do better than to have appointed Larry Potts second-in-command at the FBI.

Militias and patriot groups have been understandably ridiculed for a paranoid world-view centered on the United Nations and international banking. But ironically, many of the people doing the ridiculing share an equally paranoid world-view. Some members of the media and the gun control movement have no more idea what a real militia member is like than militia members have about what a real international banker is like. In both cases, stereotyping substitutes for understanding, and familiar devils (the United Nations for the militia, the National Rifle Association for the establishment media) are claimed to be the motive force behind the actions of a man who (allegedly) believes that the government put a microchip in his buttocks.

Nearly twenty years ago, an article in the Public Interest explained the American gun control conflict:

"[U]nderlying the gun control struggle is a fundamental division in our nation. The intensity of passion on this issue suggests to me that we are experiencing a sort of low-grade war going on between two alternative views of what America is and ought to be. On the one side are those who take bourgeois Europe as a model of a civilized society: a society just, equitable, and democratic; but well ordered, with the lines of authority clearly drawn, and with decisions made rationally and correctly by intelligent men for the entire nation. To such people, hunting is atavistic, personal violence is shameful, and uncontrolled gun ownership is a blot upon civilization."

"On the other side is a group of people who do not tend to be especially articulate or literate, and whose world view is rarely expressed in print. Their model is that of the independent frontiersman who takes care of himself and his family with no interference from the state. They are "conservative" in the sense that they cling to America's unique pre-modern tradition—a non-feudal society with a sort of medieval liberty at large for every man. To these people, "sociological" is an epithet. Life is tough and competitive. Manhood means responsibility and caring for your own."

The author explained the disaster that America will create for itself if people in government attempt to "crack down" on fearful gun-owners, thereby fulfilling the worst fears that each group has of the other:

"As they [the gun-owners] say to a man, 'I'll bury my guns in the wall first.' They ask, because they do not understand the other side, 'Why do these people want to disarm us?' They consider themselves no threat to anyone; they are not criminals, not revolutionaries. But slowly, as they become politicized, they find an analysis that fits the phenomenon they experience: Someone fears their having guns, someone is afraid of their defending their families, property, and liberty. Nasty things may happen if these people begin to feel that they are cornered.

It would be useful, therefore, if some of the mindless passion, on both side, could be drained out of the gun-control issue. Gun control is no solution to the crime problem, to the assassination problem, to the terrorist problem.... So long as the issue is kept at a white heat, with everyone having some ground to suspect everyone else's ultimate intentions, the rule of reasonableness has little chance to assert itself."

Morris Dees of the Southern Poverty Law Center has begun promoting a federal ban on group firearms training which is not authorized by state law. First of all, state governments are perfectly capable of banning or authorizing whatever they want. The proposal for a federal ban amounts to asking Washington for legislation similar to that which various allies of Mr. Dees promoted at the state level in the 1980s, with little success. The majority of states having rejected a training ban, the federal government should hardly impose the will of the minority on the rest of the states.

A former direct-mail fund-raiser for the anti-gun lobby, Mr. Dees may be forgiven for a low level of concern for the exercise of the right to keep and bear arms. But the right to keep and bear arms necessarily includes the right to practice with them, just as the Constitutional right to read a newspaper editorial about political events necessarily includes the right to learn how to read. Just as the government may not forbid people from learning how to read in groups, it may not forbid people from learning how to use firearms in groups.

"Government is the great teacher," Justice Brandeis told us. Without the unjustifiable, illegal, militaristic, deadly federal violence at Ruby Ridge and at Waco, there would be no militia movement. The federal government should set a better example. If Ruby Ridge had led to a real investigation and corrective measures—instead of years of cover-up by both the Bush and Clinton administrations—then we would not be in the current situation.

Ruby Ridge and the Waco tragedies were not the fault of a few bad officials, but the inevitable result of a culture of lawlessness, militarization, and violence that has permeated far too much of the federal law enforcement establishment. When corrective measures are undertaken—as a coalition ranging from the American Civil Liberties Union to the Citizens Committee for the Right to Keep and Bear Arms has suggested—then we will see a massive reduction in the tension between millions of American people and their government.

Turnabout Is Fair Play[4]

The old political blocs, frozen during the Cold War, really are break-ing up, as the events following the Oklahoma City bombing showed. In some respects there has been an almost comic reversal of allegiance; President Clinton, the croaking mouthpiece of liberal-ism, has been talking up law-and-order. Conservatives have been reminding us of our civil liberties. "No one has the right to run law enforcement officers down," Mr. Clinton said at one point. Don't have the right, Mr. President? Er, what does the ACLU have to say about that? I checked some recent issues of the *Nation* magazine, and Alexander Cockburn seemed positively perky about right-wing disenchantment with federal law enforcement.

The "official" news media have begun to worry about...the media. All those awful people out there are beginning to communi-cate with one another without asking anyone's permission! That is more or less the complaint of *Washington Post* columnist Jessica Mathews, who worries about "our over-faxed society." Thank you, communications revolution. The attempts by *New York Times* columnist Frank Rich to "connect the dots" between anti-abortion-ists and right-wing groups brought to mind analogous attempts by the John Birch Society to connect up the left-wing dots.

The National Rifle Association discovered "a sickening pattern of sexual harassment" and "institutional racism" within the ranks of the Bureau of Alcohol, Tobacco and Firearms. So now we oppose sickening patterns. Anthony Lewis of the *Times* reminded us that "the First Amendment gives us responsibility along with free-dom"—just the kind of thing Reed Irvine of Accuracy in Media used to say. The Oklahoma City bombing, Lewis added, makes us think about the "consequences" of hateful speech. That's funny, I don't remember him saying that at the time of the 4,000-odd bombings by the Weathermen and related groups in 1969-70. He was too busy excoriating U.S. policy makers in Vietnam to worry about the con-sequences of speech. Lewis, who has often accused people of hate without evidence, now realizes that "words matter."

"Ideas Have Consequences" used to be the quintessential conser-vative slogan. It was long repudiated by liberals, who thought ideas were "persecuted" and denied that legitimizing pornography and irresponsibility (via welfare) would affect the wider culture. Now they point to Newt Gingrich's comment that Democrats are "the enemy of normal Americans, "and remind us that opinion leaders are responsible for "the consequences" of their words. We'll buy that.

Oklahoma reminded me of conversations in the 1960s. America was so sick and racist that trying to change the law was futile, some

4Article by Tom Bethell, *The American Spectator*'s Washington correspondent, from *The American Spectator* 28:16 Jl 1, '95. Copyright © 1995 *The American Spectator*. Reprinted with permission.

said. Don't give up, the liberals would reply. "Work within the system." That's what I find myself saying today: "Work for change
within the system." Meanwhile, liberals seek to preserve their
"gains": the massive expansion of federal power they engineered
over the last sixty years. They may have been critical in the past,
but now is the time for all good lefties to come to the aid of Big
Brother, Ellen Willis said in the *Village Voice*. The post–Cold War
idea that the right was in disarray because it had lost its enemy may
have been wishful thinking by liberals.

President Clinton seized the opportunity to appeal to patriotism,
but with an inappropriate argument. "There is nothing patriotic
about…pretending that you can love your country but despise your
government," he said at Michigan State. Oh? Peggy Noonan put it
best, on NBC's "Today" show: "Americans love their country and
fear their government. Liberals love their government and fear the
people." (By the way, I have heard it said that in light of recent
rhetoric Dr. Johnson's famous adage should be amended:
Scoundrels find refuge today not in patriotism but in children—
whom budget cuts will hurt the most.) As the *Wall Street Journal*
noted, Clinton himself once claimed a patriotic basis for anti-government sentiment, in his 1969 letter to the Arkansas ROTC director. The draft system was "illegitimate," he said, because no government "should have the power to make its citizens fight and kill
and die in a war they may oppose…"

"Since the 1930s, the Commerce Clause has been one of the most important rationales for the centralization of power in Washington."

He was right about that, but he should realize that the government over which he presides has illegitimate features. The federal
government has steadily accumulated a vast amount of unconstitutional power over the last sixty years, with the connivance of judiciary and press. Until this usurpation has been corrected, patriotic
Americans will continue to fear their government. It's a measure of
the extent to which the Constitution has been subverted that liberals no longer need amend the document in order to achieve anything they want. Responding to the liberal will, Supreme Court jus-
tices have acted as *federales*, imposing federal law on the states,
overturning state law at will, and almost always waving congressional enactments through the constitutional checkpoint without a
second glance. On term limits, they once again acted as the
Beltway's reliable ally.

There was admittedly a rare exception in April. The Court ruled
5-4 that the Commerce Clause of the U.S. Constitution was insuffi-
cient justification for a federal law outlawing gun possession near
schools…. "The High Court Loses Restraint," the *New York Times*
angrily responded. Restraint? That's one way of describing what the
Court has been doing for these many years—cracking down on the
states and giving the Congress carte blanche. Since the 1930s, the
Commerce Clause has been one of the most important rationales for
the centralization of power in Washington. Its abandonment would
indeed be counterrevolutionary, but that would be too much to
hope for.

In May, George Bush emerged in his true colors. First he agreed that the GOP should drop its anti-abortion plank, then he won a round of easy applause by attacking the NRA. Clinton followed suit, reminding us that we are in the second half of the Bush-Clinton administration, and that for years we had something close to a one-party system in Washington. Some things admittedly never change. The Oklahoma City bombing was a disaster and therefore construed as an opportunity to expand federal power. New anti-terrorist legislation would have to be rushed through Congress as quickly as possible.

SCENE: The White House
> *Aide*, entering Oval Office: "Mr. President, we have a disaster..."
> *President:* "Increase federal power! What did you say the disaster was?"
> *Aide:* "Some people think the Feds have too much power, and..."
> *President:* "Increase it all the more!"

Abe Rosenthal of the *New York Times* drew attention to one of the great modern-day political asymmetries. Liberals have had the luxury of "no enemies to the left." Fidel Castro, for example, is no better than a mass murderer, but liberals risked nothing by admiring his good intentions, his alleged health-care achievements, his soaring literacy rates. Notice Castro's royal progress through the higher Parisian echelons recently. Liberals could nonchalantly share the podium with guerrilla leaders from El Salvador and members of the Communist Party. "Guilt by association" was strictly forbidden. Any attempt to connect those dots was called McCarthyism.

Conservatives, on the other hand, have been expected to repudiate anyone to their right. That's the world we have lived in for decades. Now Rosenthal worries that conservatives are daring to copy the liberals: "No enemies to the Right." It seems we do now *have* a right, which is a novelty. Personally, I don't regard them as my enemies, although I do disagree with them. They have no power of coercion, no desire to spend my money or take my property. They do not accuse me of greed, tell me whom I may or may not associate with, contribute to the delinquency of minors, or pose incessantly as my moral tutors. Those armed with legal powers are bound to be more of a threat than those with firearms alone, as we saw at Waco, and Ruby Ridge, Idaho.

True, those on the far right often are terribly misguided—believing in a U.N. plot to take over the United States, for example. In reality the U.N. is a waning institution—a cushy sinecure for the politically well connected. Rightists would be closer to the truth if they saw it as a tool of the U.S. rather than the reverse. The far right also believes some sad, poignant things, such as the existence of a plan to rescind the U.S. Constitution—as though it were not already in tatters.

We should also remember that those who disparage U.N. plots to take over the U.S. are precisely the people who hoped that one day the U.N. would take over not just the U.S. but the whole world, and do so openly. Jessica Matthews's ridicule of conspiracies to "make the nation states disappear" would be more persuasive if she had not herself argued that climate change and other "trends" are "undermining sovereignty in ways we cannot restore."

It's not so much the notion of a one-world goal as the conspiratorial attainment of it that leaves liberals aghast with disbelief. And rightly so, for those in power have no need of conspiracies. With the law on your side, you can proceed legally. Right-wingers are deluded indeed if they think their opposition is so hemmed in by the law that it is reduced to clandestine and illegal subterfuges. The shoe is more nearly on the other foot.

Repeatedly, conservatives have denounced the Oklahoma City bombing as a shocking and immoral act. What I have not seen is any acknowledgment by liberals that maybe the federal government has accumulated too much power, and needs to back off. Clinton's response has been entirely along the lines of: "How dare they suggest... How dare they criticize..." He has been surprisingly partisan—openly on the side of Big Brother and the recipient classes. These admittedly were the people who voted for him. Unlike Bush, he has the political sense to shore up his own base. For two months Clinton has been moving to the left rather than the center, obviously heading off a challenge from within his own party. There has been little acknowledgment that he is, as they used to say, president of all the people.

What all this tells me is that the liberals, unlike the Communists, are not going to give up without a fight. They have long intended to re-educate us, remake our lives, shape our thoughts, our habits, and our bank balances, and they are not about to abandon the effort just because the country is in what they see as a "cynical" mood. We, of course, will keep pressing for peaceful change, working within the system. As we do so, let us bear in mind the words of John F. Kennedy: "Those who make peaceful change impossible will make violent change inevitable."

Liberalism and Terror[5]

For American liberals, Thomas Jefferson is the cultural hero *par excellence*, cherished for his positions on freedom of expression and on separation of Church and State and for his populistic rhetoric. (That this was a populism for whites only is a fact which American liberals have managed not to address.)

Of course Jefferson is a hero to many Americans apart from liberals, and his admirers include, as we now know, some white right-wing terrorists. On July 3, 1995, the *Washington Post* published Serge Kovaleski's profile of Terry Lynn Nichols, the second man charged in the Oklahoma City bombing. According to Kovaleski, Nichols read the works of Thomas Jefferson and Thomas Paine and was particularly inspired by Jefferson's maxim, "The tree of liberty must be refreshed from time to time with the blood of patriots and tyrants."

According to CNN News (January 31, 1996), the first suspect in the Oklahoma City bombing, Timothy McVeigh, was wearing a T-shirt carrying those same words at the time he was arrested while driving away from Oklahoma City. The CNN correspondent, Susan Candiotti, put a question about the T-shirt to McVeigh's lawyer, Stephen Jones. Jones replied: "Well, if Thomas Jefferson said it, I don't think it would be incriminating at all."

Jefferson did say it. He wrote those words in a letter to William Stevens Smith on November 13, 1787. Jefferson was writing from Paris, where he was Minister Pleniportentiary at the time, but the words do not imply any premonition of impending revolution in France. They are used in justification of Shays's Rebellion in Massachusetts. In the letter to Smith, the words, "It is its natural manure," appear after "blood of patriots and tyrants."

Jefferson did not have the French Revolution in mind when he wrote those words. But as soon as that revolution began he wrote about it in the "tree of liberty" spirit, and set virtually no limits to the amount of blood the French Revolutionaries might legitimately shed in the cause of liberty—" Rather than it should have failed, I would have seen half the earth desolated." So Jefferson wrote in January 1793 after the news of the September massacres in Paris had reached America.

The concept of the bloodthirsty tree of liberty entered into the rhetoric of the French Revolution itself and specifically into the rhetoric of the Revolutionary Terror. The terrorist Bertrand Barère used a variant of it in the peroration of his speech calling for the execution of Louis XVI: "The tree of liberty, as an ancient author remarks, flourishes when it is watered with the blood of all varieties of tyrants." Macaulay, whose knowledge of classical literature was

---

[5]Article by Conor Cruise O'Brien, author of *The Long Affair: Thomas Jefferson and the French Revolution, 1785–1800*, from *National Review* 48:29-30+ Ap 22, '96. Copyright © 1996 NATIONAL REVIEW, Inc. Reprinted with permission.

prodigious, did not believe in the existence of Barère's "ancient author": "In the course of our own small reading among the Greek and Latin writers, we have not happened to fall in with trees of liberty and watering-pots full of blood, nor can we, such is our ignorance of classical ambiguity, even imagine an Attic or Roman orator employing imagery of that sort" (*Edinburgh Review*, April 1844).

We know (as Macaulay probably did not) that Thomas Jefferson had "employed imagery of that sort" five years before Barère did and in the same city. Could the idea have reached Barère from Jefferson? Conceivably. Barère could not have known of Jefferson's letter of five years before to an American correspondent. But Jefferson had been in Paris for the Fall of the Bastille, which was accompanied and followed by a number of bloody episodes. Jefferson's dispatches and letters of the period reflect a sober appreciation of the efficiency of mob violence in a revolutionary situation. "The decapitation of de Launay worked powerfully thro' the night on the whole aristocratical party [so that they realized] the absolute necessity that the king should give up everything to the States [General]. Some of Jefferson's acquaintances in Paris (who mostly belonged, like La Rochefoucauld and Condorcet, to the Enlightenment section of the nobility) may well have been shocked by the bloodshed, and have said so to Jefferson. If so, he could well have comforted them with some version of the thought about the tree of liberty and its natural manure. The story could then have gone the rounds and eventually reached the ears which were most likely to be attracted by the characteristics of that tree.

In any case, the bloodthirsty tree remains part of the revolutionary and terrorist traditions in the twentieth century. In "The Rose Tree"—the most "revolutionary" of the four poems W. B. Yeats wrote about the Easter Rising of 1916—the last stanza runs:

> *"But where can we draw water,"*
> *Said Pearse to Connolly,*
> *"When all the wells are parched away?*
> *O plain as plain can be*
> *There's nothing but our own red blood*
> *Can make a right Rose Tree."*

Yeats was probably not aware of the Jeffersonian origins of his metaphor. But I have heard the Jeffersonian passage about the tree correctly quoted, and properly attributed, by people who were interested in legitimizing the terror offensive of the Provisional IRA, which began in 1971, was suspended in 1994, and again resumed in February of this year.

Liberalism and terrorism appear as opposing concepts. But they have something in common. Both belong to the large and heterogeneous family of the devotees of freedom. Freedom is the most powerful and the most ambiguous of abstract ideas. There are two main divisions within the massive ambiguities. There is freedom

"...the Provisional IRA, which began in 1971, was suspended in 1994, and again resumed in February of this year."

combined with order and limited by law. This is the freedom of England's Glorious Revolution and of the American Constitution. This is the "manly, moral, regulated liberty" which Burke defended in *Reflections on the Revolution in France*. This is the freedom of the mainstream liberal tradition in the English-speaking world. And it is also the freedom of the mainstream *conservative* tradition in the same world. In their philosophy of freedom, the common ground between the two traditions is more important than the differences. Edmund Burke belongs to both those traditions, and no one should seek to wrest him from one of them in order to monopolize him for the other.

Outside the zone of ordered freedom, now more or less coextensive with the Western world, the idea of freedom and the love of freedom take starker and more elemental forms. Freedom is thought of as the appurtenance and rightful heritage of a particular group of people defined by nationality, religion, language, ancestry, or territorial affiliation, and usually by some combination of several of these elements. Some other group or groups of people are felt to be denying freedom to us, who must have it. Freedom so understood is one of the most powerful of human motivating forces and the most destructive, impelling large numbers of people to risk their lives for it and to take the lives of others, the enemies of freedom. Serbs and Croats cut one another's throats, and all for freedom's sake.

"Russians are making a brave effort to establish an ordered version of freedom..."

When the Communist system collapsed in Europe, many Westerners were confident that freedom would take its place, and so it did. But in many parts of the former Soviet Union, the freedom that emerged was not freedom as understood in the West, but rather a conflict of freedoms: national and ethnic freedoms, at war with one another. Russians are making a brave effort to establish an ordered version of freedom, but that version is challenged by other versions.

Much of the world today breathes what Edmund Burke called "the wild *gas*" of liberty. Burke used that phrase about the French Revolution in the condition it was in 1790, a year after the Fall of the Bastille, and two years before the advent of the Terror. The Whigs—the ancestors of modern liberals—believed that the French Revolution was over, having brought about the triumph of liberty. Burke was about to break with the Whigs, over that proposition. He wrote in *Reflections*:

> "When I see the spirit of liberty in action, I see a strong principle at work; and this, for a while, is all I can know of it. The wild *gas*, the fixed air is plainly broke loose; but we ought to suspend our judgment until the first effervescence is a little subdued, till the liquor is cleared and until we see something deeper than the agitation of a troubled and frothy surface. I must be tolerably sure before I venture publicly to congratulate men upon a blessing that they have really received one. I should therefore suspend my congrat-

ulations on the new liberty of France, until I was informed how it had been combined with government, which public force, with the discipline and obedience of armies, with the collection of an effective and well-distributed revenue; with morality and religion; with the solidity of property; with peace and order; with civil and social manners. All these (in their way) are good things too, and, without them, liberty is not a benefit in itself, and is not likely to continue long. The effect of liberty to individuals is, that they may do what they please. We ought to see what it will please them to do, before we risk congratulations, which may soon be turned into complaints."

I referred just now to the contrast between "ordered liberty" in the West, and passionate versions of liberty in the world outside. The contrast is obvious, but it is not clear cut. Within the West also there are passionate absolutist libertarians claiming inspiration from within the Western tradition, as in the cases of the persons arrested for the Oklahoma City bombing. And Western liberals are ill-prepared to cope with terrorism. This is a question of psychology, not of formal liberal doctrine. In the British tradition that doctrine was formulated most authoritatively by John Stuart Mill in *On Liberty*. Mill wrote: "The sole end for which mankind are warranted, individually or collectively, in interfering with the liberty of action of any of their number, is self-protection." The doctrine of "self-protection" would seem to authorize democratic societies to take such measures as may be necessary to defend the citizens against terrorist conspiracies, without defection from liberal principles. If the ordinary courts, and the ordinary criminal laws, are inadequate to protect the citizens from terrorism, then a liberal of the school of Mill could legislate, without a qualm of principle, for the introduction of internment without trial of persons whom the security authorities believe to be terrorists.

John Stuart Mill is the leading British liberal *thinker*. But a figure more representative of the British liberal tradition is the great liberal *politician*, William Ewart Gladstone. And Gladstone is the classic embodiment of the weakness of the English liberal mind in trying to cope with terrorism. Gladstone admitted that his whole attitude to Ireland was changed overnight by a single Irish terrorist act: the Fenian bombing of Clerkenwell Prison in 1867. That bomb convinced Gladstone that the Irish must be suffering from terrible grievances, which it was his duty to remove. "My mission is to pacify Ireland," he declared. He tried to do this by a series of reforms, beginning with the disestablishment of the Irish (Anglican) Church in 1870.

The Irish terrorists were not interested in matters like Church disestablishment. But they were very interested in the effect which their Clerkenwell bomb had had on the mind of the leading British politician of the day. What Gladstone's reaction to that bomb taught them was that terrorism *works*. And that lesson is the most enduring legacy of Gladstonian liberalism. "Violence is the only thing the British understand" is the favorite maxim of Irish Republicans even today. Canary Wharf in 1996 is heir to Clerkenwell in 1867.

At the level of logic, the liberal mind is in the grip of a fallacy: that terrorism can be rooted out by concessions and compromise, without any need to resort to inconvenient and painful emergency measures, like internment. This is a fallacy, because the terrorist mind is absolutist and unappeasable. Irish terrorists want to destroy Northern Ireland, and will not voluntarily stop anywhere short of that. Arab terrorists want to destroy Israel, and will not voluntarily stop anywhere short of that. Both sets of terrorists are interested in concessions and efforts at compromise only as evidence that the bombings are moving the enemy in the right direction, however slowly.

Compromises are possible, of course, but only with terrorists who are willing to become ex-terrorists, like Michael Collins in the 1920s or Arafat now. But terrorism survived the compromises. In the current case, Israel surrendered territory to Arafat, hoping to get peace in exchange. But unreconstructed terrorists, ignoring Arafat, have been able to use the territory surrendered as a base for attacks on Israel.

"The total active membership of the IRA is reckoned as between two and three thousand."

To seek to end terrorism by compromise is a fallacy in logic, because it misrepresents the nature of the phenomenon with which it attempts to cope. But beneath the fallacy lies a powerful emotional force: guilt (exceptionally strong in Gladstone, for example). British Gladstonian liberals—to be found today among both Tories and Labourites feel chronically guilty about Britain's past treatment of Ireland. Israeli doves—the liberals of Israel—feel guilty about Israel's treatment of Palestinian Arabs. In both cases, there are some reasons for guilt. Unfortunately, feelings of guilt are of no help in the struggle against terrorism. On the contrary, they are a resource which the terrorist knows he can exploit, and he does so with a savage satisfaction.

In some cases, but not in all, there are political initiatives that could isolate the terrorists, and perhaps eventually lead to their defeat. For Israel, peace with Syria is the best available option: to give back the Golan Heights, in exchange for which Syria would eliminate terrorists in Lebanon and dry up the sources of supply for terrorists in the Territories.

In Northern Ireland, unfortunately, no promising political option is within reach. There are two sets of private armies there, a Protestant one and a Catholic one. Efforts to appease one—at present the Catholics—do not appease it, and they risk arousing the latent violence of the other one. Efforts to make the realities of Northern Ireland conform to a Gladstonian agenda are doomed to failure. The best hope for Northern Ireland would be a co-ordination of security measures between London and Dublin, including the introduction of internment—applied evenly to both sets of political-sectarian paramilitaries—on both sides of the border. (Which worked during the Second World War and in 1957-1962.) At present British and Irish versions of liberalism (combining in Ireland with nationalism) inhibit that response. I fear that the necessary measures will not be taken until things get much worse. The IRA promises another 25 years of "war."

If the terrorist threat increases in America, American liberals are likely to oppose any counter-measures which may be proposed against it. In doing so they will claim the sanction of Thomas Jefferson, whose protests against the Alien and Sedition Acts of 1798 are part of the charter of American liberalism. But I don't think American liberalism is strong enough, in itself, to inhibit counter-measures against terrorism. What might inhibit them is something different but cognate: the dislike among millions of Americans for the restraints and constraints of "ordered freedom" and a taste for the absolute stuff, straight out of the bottle: the version of the Jeffersonian tradition offered by McVeigh and Nichols. Most of the five million members of the National Rifle Association no doubt repudiate terrorist acts. But most of them would oppose any serious clampdown on terrorists who happened to be white, Christian, and conservative. So liberals protesting against an anti-terrorist clampdown would have some unaccustomed allies. If American terrorism ever acquires sustained momentum, it could be more dangerous than is today's terrorism in the Middle East and the British Isles.

Let me close with a pair of disquieting statistics. I have seen it estimated that there are between thirty and forty thousand armed men in the militia movement who regard themselves as either at war or on the verge of war with the Federal Government. The total active membership of the IRA is reckoned as between two and three thousand.

II. The Terrorist and the Terrorist Action

Editor's Introduction

Regrettably, it appears that the increase of terrorism in the United States reflects an increase in the number of American groups and individuals who feel that violent action is the only means of expression open to them. In general, American terrorist actions are committed by relatively organized militias or by religious extremists. Yet, as these articles will reveal, many individuals who commit such actions are neither part of an organized group nor particularly radical or extremist in their beliefs; they are simply striving to achieve a greater and more direct level of control over their immediate environment.

In Article one, entitled "Restaking the Claim," from *American Forests,* Herbert E. McLean discusses the actions of Western coalitions and individuals who believe that the U.S. government has no constitutional right to own or manage forest land. McLean describes Western Americans as, in general, preferring local to federal authority and as supportive of such organizations as the States' Rights Home Rule Movement, which encourages civil disobedience in these matters. The movement may be nonviolent but the controversy is not: Forest Service stations have been bombed and employees of the agency harassed and threatened.

"The Other Fundamentalists," by Steven Emerson from *The New Republic,* examines militant Muslim factions in the United States which are often accused of terrorist activities. Although these groups deny any involvement in terrorism, the author notes that they possess large sums of money, weapons, and explosives. In addition, their publications are full of diatribes against Israel and its ally, the U.S., and praise terrorist actions as legitimate tactics in a holy war.

The third article, "Militia Movement: Prescription for Disaster," by Thomas Halpren, David Rosenberg, and Irwin Suall, explores the presence of militia groups within the U.S. The authors cite evidence which indicates that organized and often violent groups have continued to grow, even after the Oklahoma City bombing. Increasingly these groups are making use of advanced technology to reach a wider audience. The authors present a state-by-state summary of militia activity in the U.S.

James Brooke, writing in *The New York Times*, examines the Viper Militia, an anti-government paramilitary group. The Viper Militia is prepared to fight the Federal Government and "take action against the families of the [federal] agents who took action against them." Six of the twelve Viper Militia members have been arrested and charged with conspiracy to blow up local, state, and federal buildings in Phoenix, Arizona. The author describes their extensive training, which involves both explosives and guns, and calls their methods typical and their membership reflective of the overall "demographics of the anti-government paramilitary movement."

The final article, "Antiabortion Extremists: Organized and Dangerous," reprinted from *Glamour* magazine, describes abortion clinics as the most common targets of bombings in America today. (This article is particularly timely in light of the double-bombing of an abortion clinic in Atlanta in January 1997.) In addition to "clinic violence," the author cites instances of antiabortion vandalism and the stalking of doctors who perform abortions.

Restaking the Claim[1]

A county commissioner in remote Nye County, Nevada, climbs aboard a D-7 bulldozer and reopens 400 feet of closed road within Toiyabe National Forest, as a Fourth of July crowd watches with admiration. In the process, he nearly mows down two Forest Service special agents—sent to prevent the illegal action—standing in front of the 'dozer.

On Tongass National Forest in Alaska, two Tlingit native youths, banished by tribal leaders to a "remote island" after robbing and beating a pizza delivery man, illegally occupy land and use firearms.

Eight men are convicted of planting enough explosives in Quartzite Falls, on Arizona's Tonto National Forest, to blast the once-Class 6 rapids to benign status—apparently to facilitate rafting (and boost revenues therefrom) through the pristine Salt River Canyon Wilderness.

"...States, not the federal government own all forestlands..."

Folks with high passions and different designs upon the land are increasingly entering our national forests. They're testing the Forest Service's time-honored slogan. "Land of Many Uses," to the limit in what appears to be a growing push for "home rule."

Today's point man in that movement is Nevada county commissioner/bulldozer operator Richard Carver, whose mom and dad opened a modest restaurant and bar deep in the Nevada desert in 1938. His claim: States, not the federal government own all forestlands, including the Toiyabe National Forest, and local counties like Nye have authority to manage them. He persuasively waves a copy of the U.S. Constitution to sell his point, while vehemently denying even the *existence* a national forest.

Leaders of the so-called States' Rights Home Rule Movement, which is gathering steam in the West, gather crowds of sometimes several hundred in outlying communities in a mode similar to the Sagetbrush Rebellion of the 80s. Espousing a nonviolent approach while urging civil disobedience and calling all environmental laws "unconstitutional," leaders clamor for a return of power "to the people," usually meaning county governments.

"We're bringing the feds to their knees," Carver proclaimed to *American Forests* this spring.

Last July after the bulldozing incident, and under the local banner of the Nevada Plan for Public lands, Commissioner Carver filed criminal charges against a Forest Service law-enforcement special agent who, with an agency district ranger, had come to protect a nearby slice of Toiyabe Forest where Carver was preparing to open a closed road. The charge: "impersonating a peace officer."

With a bomb exploding at a ranger station in Carson City, Nevada, this spring (no injuries but plenty of structural damage), a second

---

[1]Article by Herbert E. McLean, from *American Forests* 101:24 + Jl/Ag '95. Copyright © 1995 Herbert E. McLean. Reprinted with permission.

bomb exploding in an outhouse in neighboring Humbolt National Forest, and a bomb threat received at Toiyabe Forest headquarters near Reno early in April, tensions were high, but Carver was claiming no responsibility.

He told *American Forest* that the Forest Service planted the Carson City bombs, but offered no evidence.

"They want to make us look stupid, but we got some pretty good publicity out of it," Carver reported.

The Forest Service—adopting a nonconfrontational mode, though it fervently hoped to defuse a potential time-bomb out West—has filed suit to get a fresh legal opinion on just who owns our national forests, quoting chapter and verse on federal statutes already in place. And though several small Nevada newspapers are carrying the home-rule banner, larger metropolitan dailies are treading lightly or calling for a return to reason.

"For the Nye County commissioners to seize a national forest makes as much sense as having the city of New York seize the Statue of Liberty," the *Seattle Post-Intelligencer* recently editorialized.

Meanwhile, most Forest Service employees out West aren't carrying sidearms, as they might have in decades past, but rather wallet-size "crisis cards" telling them what to do if they're arrested by local authorities. Threatening, resisting, or interfering with a Forest Service employee is a federal crime, the card tells them summarily. The FBI will investigate.

Following the catastrophic bombing assault on lives and federal property in Oklahoma in mid-April, it's a good bet that any threats or gestures portending violence—bulldozers included—will be dealt with considerably more resolutely than in the past. And that kind of law enforcement may require a lot more than an instruction card in a federal employee's hip pocket. In Alaska, those "banished" youths, who have been living in two spartan, separated cabins on Tongass National Forest, are apparently now being used in support of larger causes: to test Tlingit native claims of primordial land use, and thus ownership, in Southeast Alaska.

"Our fathers and forefathers...have lived on and occupied Kuiu Island until the memory of man runneth not to the contrary," a tribal judge is reported as saying.

The boys' use of firearms and occupancy of land without a Forest Service permit seriously concern the Forest Service, which has been working for years to build good relations with local native tribes. A number of such groups received large tracts under the Alaska Native Claims Settlement Act of 1971.

A hoped-for solution: The banished boys quietly move to another area outside national-forest boundaries to serve out their banishment.

As for the river blasters in Arizona, their case is simpler: The "Quartzite Eight" were summarily arrested and have pleaded guilty to felony charges of destroying government property The "powder man" was fined $15,000 this spring and is now serving a year in the clink.

The Other Fundamentalists[2]

We know, after the Oklahoma City bombing, that terrorism in the United States can take many forms, domestic and foreign, populist and insurrectionist, from those with bizarre domestic grudges to those with radical foreign agendas. The growing awareness of this threat is part of what motivated the closing of Pennsylvania Avenue in front of the White House last week. Until Oklahoma City, the consensus in the FBI was that, of the various extremist groups in the United States, it was radical Islamist groups that most gravely threaten American security. And for all the new evidence of domestic terrorism, that judgment remains the same.

Over the past year alone, the FBI has created dozens of special units around the country—with hundreds of agents and analysts—whose tasks include tracking these radical Islamist groups.

A two-year investigation I recently concluded helps show why the government is so concerned. The investigation—which involved hundreds of interviews with moderate and militant Islamist officials and with law enforcement and intelligence officials, as well as the acquisition of more than 150,000 documents, publications and recordings produced by radical Islamist groups—revealed that these groups have established elaborate political, financial and, in some cases, operational infrastructures in the United States. Because of the scope of this movement (it ranges from New York to Oklahoma to California), its bellicose rhetoric (it calls for a holy war or "jihad" against the U.S. and other governments) and its advocacy of terror to achieve its ends (it trains recruits in the use of car bombs), it's no wonder the FBI has made this network a top priority.

Given the FBI's limitations, however, both in resources and in legal authority to investigate groups that define themselves as religious, it could be a while before the bureau gets the upper hand. "It took the bureau more than ten years before it could infiltrate the Mafia, learn the language, recruit Sicilians," says Don Lavey, a former FBI official who served as head of Interpol's counter-terrorism branch. "But this time, the threat is much greater and the bureau's resources incredibly more limited."

Islam is the fastest growing religion in the U.S., and the vast majority of Muslims in America are peaceful and law-abiding and do not condone violence. But in recent years an extremist fringe of militant Islamism has taken root here. To avoid raising suspicion and to take advantage of civil liberties protections, these militant groups often reconstitute themselves here as "research," "charitable" or "civil rights" institutions. Ahmed Said Nasr, an Egyptian journalist and former diplomat based in Washington, has studied

[2]Article by Steven Emerson, executive producer of the PBS documentary *Jihad in America,* from *The New Republic* 212:21 Je 12, '95. Copyright © 1995 *The New Republic.* Reprinted with permission.

militant Islamist groups in the United States. "During the past several years, there has been not only a proliferation of Islamic fundamentalist groups in the United States," says Nasr, "but they have carried out a major deception to the American public by masquerading as charities and religious or educational organizations. In the West, you think of schools or religious institutions as totally innocent because of your tradition of separation of church and state. But for the Islamic fundamentalist movement there is no separation of church and state."

Oliver B. Revell, a former senior FBI official in charge of counter-terrorist and counter-intelligence investigations, puts the objectives of these groups in no uncertain terms. "They are ultimately committed to waging holy war, both in the Middle East and the world at large against all of their opposition," he says. "And that means us." Seif Ashmawi, the Egyptian-born American-based publisher of a bilingual newspaper called The Voice of Peace, concurs. "The aim of these groups," Ashmawi says, "is the same as their aim in the Middle East: to build and expand their radical religious-political empire and eliminate or discredit all their enemies, particularly Muslims like myself who don't agree with radical fundamentalists' claim to represent Islam."

"Many of these groups are willing to work together in diaspora because they feel they are surrounded by a common enemy."

Although there is no evidence that these myriad Islamist groups are centrally coordinated, it does appear that they collaborate and cross-fertilize. Evidence collected by federal investigators in the cases related to the February 26, 1993, World Trade Center bombing, for example, shows that leaders or representatives of at least five different groups—including the Palestinian-based Islamic Jihad, Hamas, the Sudanese National Islamic Front, the Pakistan-based al-Fuqrah (a black Islamist group) and groups funded by Persian Gulf donors—were involved in the plot. Sudanese diplomats affiliated with the National Islamic Front aided conspirators with access and credentials. In addition, Sheik Omar Abdul Rahman, the blind Egyptian cleric accused of being the spiritual ringleader of the World Trade Center conspiracy, had been hosted or sponsored in the U.S. by at least half a dozen mosques and innocent-sounding Islamist "charitable" and "religious" organizations. Many of these groups are willing to work together in diaspora because they feel they are surrounded by a common enemy: Westerners and their values.

Perhaps the best places to observe what brings these groups together are the Islamist conventions, held annually, often in the bland hotels and convention centers of Midwestern cities. Among the best-attended are those sponsored by the Muslim Arab Youth Association (MAYA). Founded in 1974 and headquartered in Plainfield, Indiana, MAYA has evolved into an umbrella organization for militant Islamist groups around the world. Its influence can be seen in the impressive parade of top Islamist militants who have addressed past conventions. They include Rachid al-Ghannouchi, head of the militant Tunisian al-Nahda movement (who was sentenced to death in absentia for his role in deadly terrorist attacks in Tunisia but now lives under political asylum in Britain); Mustapha

Mash'hur, the Egyptian Muslim Brotherhood deputy supreme guide; Musa Abu Marzuk, the head of Hamas's political committee, who lived in the U.S. from 1973 to 1993; Yusef al-Qaradhawi, an Egyptian Muslim Brotherhood cleric based in Qatar; Ahmad al-Qattan, a Hamas leader based in Kuwait; Sheik Ahmad Nofal, a recruiter of Hamas terrorists in Jordan; and Ibrahim Gousheh, Hamas's spokesman in Jordan.

MAYA, like its parent organization, Muslim Brotherhood, embraces the belief that Western, particularly American society, is morally corrupt, intrinsically anti-Islamic and evil. "In the heart of America, in the depths of corruption and ruin and moral depriva- tion, an elite of Muslim youth is holding fast to the teachings of Allah," states the preface to MAYA's "Constitution," which is print- ed in Arabic and distributed at its conventions. A companion pub- lication, "Guide for the Muslim Family in America," explains: "Western civilization is based upon the separation of religion from life.... Islamic civilization is based upon principles fundamentally opposed to those of Western civilization."

MAYA's conferences serve several purposes. They help conserva- tive Muslims fight the trend toward assimilation in the secular cul- ture of the United States. They rally American Muslims in support of various militant Islamist causes. They showcase and promote Islamist charities that fund militant movements abroad. They offer a pretext for some of the world's most notorious militant Islamist leaders to come to the United States and get together under the same roof, where, according to law enforcement officials, in addi- tion to addressing Muslim Americans, they divide monies raised through charities and coordinate operations behind closed doors. Finally, the conferences provide militant organizations with a cover to observe and recruit operatives in the U.S. for terrorist activities. A Chicago-based Palestinian-American who was convicted of abet- ting terrorist acts admitted to Israeli authorities, for example, that he had helped to train Hamas recruits at a MAYA convention.

At the most recent MAYA conference, held at a Hyatt hotel in Chicago in December, 5,000 people heard speech after speech asserting that Muslims around the globe were under bitter attack. The attendees were told that, as the vanguard of the Muslim Ummah (or "nation"), they were required to reclaim Islam's lost glory. In addition to a few non-political sermons, one could also hear vehement denunciations of Israel and the PLO-Israeli accords, describing them as modern-day equivalents of the anti-Muslim Crusades. Greeting the conventioneers was the headline of MAYA's Arabic-language newspaper: "Jihad in America: The Crusades Continue!"—a reference to a film I produced for PBS last year on militant Islamist groups in the U.S.

Men and women, most dressed in traditional scarves, were segre- gated in accordance with Islamic law, though in the halls and ele- vators, the sexes mixed. Perhaps half of the conference-goers were younger than 20. On a floor below the conference rooms was a bazaar, set up wall-to-wall with bookstalls, tables and stands selling delicacies, children's books, religious texts, baseball hats and t-shirts embroidered with slogans like "Islam Is the Solution." At other stalls, relief organizations collected donations for the Muslim victims of "Genocide," the "crusades" and other forms of repression in Palestine, Bosnia, the Philippines, Egypt, Algeria and elsewhere. The makeshift marketplace was also well-stocked with books on Jews, including several editions of the *Protocols of the Elders of Zion* and titles such as *Freemasons' and Christians' Conspiracy Against Islam, The Myth of Jesus Christ, The Jews Are Coming, Islam and Jewish Conspiracies* and *The Dangers of Jewish Existence to the Islamic Ummah*. At the Islamic Association for Palestine table—one of the largest—books and videos lauding Hamas were in plentiful supply. One such book was dedicated to the martyrdom of Imad Aqel, a legendary Hamas terrorist who had personally killed Jews and fellow Palestinians deemed to be "collaborators" before being shot to death in a gun battle with Israeli soldiers in 1993.

Nearby, at a stand soliciting donations for the imprisoned Sheik Abdul Rahman, a young man handed out a brochure called "U.S. War on Islam and Its Scholars," which explained that the sheik's indictment was "a prelude for a U.S. government campaign against all Muslim activists" and "proof that Islam in America is targeted by the U.S. government."

Among this year's more popular lecturers was the bearded, avuncular-looking Bassam al-Amoush, a member of the Islamic coalition in the Jordanian parliament, who boasted of how his party boycotted President Bill Clinton's address to that body. "Somebody approached me at the mosque [in Amman] and asked me, 'If I see a Jew in the street, should I kill him?'" al-Amoush said, putting on a dumbfounded face. "'Don't ask me,' I said to him. 'After you kill him, come and tell me.'" The crowd roared with laughter. "What do you want from me, a fatwa [religious ruling]? Really, a good deed does not require one."

Minutes later, a message was handed to the master of ceremonies, who read it aloud. A hush fell over the conference room as he announced: "We have very good news. There was an attack on a bus in Jerusalem, perpetrated by a Palestinian policeman. Nineteen were wounded and three were killed. Hamas has taken responsibility for the act." (This was on December 26, when a Hamas suicide bomber blew up a bus in downtown Jerusalem. It was later revealed that only the bomber died; twelve Israelis were wounded.) The crowd responded with shouts of "Allahu Akbar!"

For al-Amoush, like other militant Islamist leaders before him, the visit to the United States provided an opportunity to raise morale and support among American Muslims for the Islamist movement worldwide. Here, unlike in his native land, al-Amoush doesn't have to worry about the authorities clamping down on him. In Jordan, members of his Islamic coalition had come under sharp scrutiny after Jordanian police uncovered their involvement in an assassination plot against King Hussein and in efforts to supply weapons to Hamas for attacks on Israel. In the United States, he can speak without worry. Six months earlier, he addressed a smaller gathering of fundamentalists in Detroit, where he assured his listeners that it was "certainly possible to defeat America, as the Vietnamese demonstrated." He declared America "the number one enemy and...the Great Satan."

Despite this anti-American rhetoric, al-Amoush was, on another occasion last fall, received by staff of the Senate Foreign Relations Committee, as well as by State Department officials. This series of meetings was arranged by the Committee on American Islamic Relations, a fledgling organization that promotes the interests of militant Islam in the U.S. In meeting with al-Amoush, the American officials were not seeking to legitimize him or his coalition; rather, they were conforming to a policy of establishing low-level diplomatic contacts with groups all along the Islamist spectrum, in order to round out America's assessment of the Middle East. However reasonable the motives, though, such contacts have proved problematic: two years ago, for example, similar meetings held in Egypt with Muslim Brotherhood representatives and in Jordan with Hamas officials were stopped after protests by the respective governments.

"The trooper found a small arsenal of semi-automatic weapons and several out-of-state license plates in the trunk."

Many times, the incendiary speech heard at Islamist conventions remains simply an outlet for frustration and a reminder of long-standing grievances. But over the past few years, it has at times, in the eyes of a few zealots, become a call for waging a kind of holy war in the U.S. One of the first indications that a militant fringe was preparing for jihad on U.S. soil was an incident that took place on August 29, 1989. That day, according to FBI documents, a Connecticut state trooper stopped a vehicle carrying six "Middle Eastern persons" near the High Rock Shooting Range in Naugatuck, Connecticut. The trooper found a small arsenal of semi-automatic weapons and several out-of-state license plates in the trunk. The guns belonged to the driver, a local gun dealer and former Waterbury policeman of Albanian origin, who said he was training volunteers to fight against the Soviets in Afghanistan. Since the weapons were legally licensed, no arrests were made. A computer check found, however, that the extra license plates were registered to El-Sayyid Nosair, who later was arrested for the shooting on November 5, 1990, of militant Jewish leader Rabbi Meir Kahane. After that shooting, the police found in Nosair's possession a gun license registered in the name of the same former Waterbury cop who was driving the car in August 1989.

Weapons training was apparently not an uncommon practice among Nosair's colleagues, who, according to FBI reports, used at least six different shooting ranges. At the range in Connecticut, a 1990 FBI report says, they would "shoot 1,000 rounds a day at silhouette-shaped targets." Religious leaders apparently attended such sessions as well, including Sheik Tamimi al-Adnani, one of the two top commanders of the volunteer movement to support the Jihad in Afghanistan.

More than two years earlier, FBI informants had reported seeing weapons in the al-Farouq Mosque in Brooklyn. But an application for a wiretap on the mosque was denied by the Justice Department. Since any escalation of the probe could be seen as violating federal guidelines that require advance evidence of criminal conspiracy, surveillance was first restricted and ultimately curtailed. Yet, unknown to authorities at the time, the al-Farouq Mosque had also become a center for counterfeiting tens of thousands of dollars, shipping bomb components to Hamas in Israel, reconfiguring passports to enable Muslim volunteers to visit the U.S. and enlisting new recruits for the worldwide jihad.

In those days before the World Trade Center bombing, the FBI was sometimes caught off guard by the Islamist threat. On November 6, 1990, hours after Nosair was arrested for the murder of Kahane, police raided his New Jersey apartment and carted away forty-seven boxes of personal papers. But because much of it was in Arabic and deemed "irrelevant, religious" material, the contents were shelved until days after the World Trade Center bombing. When leads in the investigation of the bombing indicated Islamist involvement, investigators returned to Nosair's cache and discovered what they had missed: a road map to an international terrorist network headquartered in the U.S., including plans he detailed in one notebook to "demoralize the enemies of Allah...by means of destroying and blowing up the pillars of their civilization and blowing up the tourist attractions they are so proud of and the high buildings they are so proud of."

Also ignored until after the bombing were cassette tapes Nosair had made of telephone conversations between the U.S.-based holy warriors and their Pakistan-based and Palestinian counterparts and leaders. In one conversation, Abdul Rahman (apparently speaking from Peshawar, Pakistan) asks his followers in New Jersey about "camps" in theUnited States. On the tape, a male voice responds, "It was a success. It started Friday evening and ended Monday. It lasted three days, and we expect positive results."

The World Trade Center conspiracy and subsequent trials have provided a rich source of materials on the extensive terrorist infrastructure in the New York and New Jersey areas. "But," says Revell, "it is only a small part of the picture. There is an extensive subterranean network in the United States of radical militants whose activities are not illegal. What we need to focus on is what these people are saying—that's the key to understanding what they will do."

Of all the Islamist militant groups active in America, Hamas has developed the most sophisticated infrastructure, complete with charitable, political, social and even military wings. The story of how a young man named Nasser Issa Jalal Hidmi was recruited and trained by Hamas shows how elaborate and sophisticated the

Hamas military network in the U.S. has become. Hidmi's story was reconstructed by studying documents retrieved by Israeli investigators and confessions to Israeli courts by various Hamas operatives.

As a student in a Jerusalem preparatory college, Hidmi joined an Islamic religious group that served as a greenhouse for future military operatives. Motivated by a strong antipathy to Israeli occupation, Hidmi soon found his way to a cleric who went by the nom de guerre of Abu 'Ubada and supervised a unit of Hamas terror squads. In a short time, Hidmi showed promise and was selected to participate in armed training in the United States, a place he had always wanted, but could never afford, to visit.

In June 1990, a few months after arriving in the U.S. and settling in Manhattan, Kansas, Hidmi received a phone call from Mohammed Salah, a Chicago-based used-car salesman who served as commander of the military wing of Hamas in the United States. (Salah has since confessed to abetting terrorist acts and is serving a five-year sentence in an Israeli prison.)

Following Salah's instructions, Hidmi flew to Chicago for a weekend of military-style training at a campground on the outskirts of the city. In this "basic training" course, Hidmi and twenty-five other young Palestinians received religious instruction. According to Hidmi's later confession, they also were taught how to plant car bombs. A Libyan-American man identifying himself as a former Marine explained to the group, using charts and diagrams, where to place a bomb in a car's engine and how to ensure its detonation at the point of ignition. Following this instruction, the recruits returned home.

Later that year, Hidmi and the other Hamas inductees were told to attend an Islamist convention in Kansas City. Over the next three days, they listened as top Hamas officials spoke of their pride in the organization and in the international Islamist movement, and railed against the Zionist conspiracy. Musa Abu Marzuk, the international political chief of Hamas, who was living in Louisiana at the time, called upon all Muslims to destroy the "outpost of Western influence" that was created with the "purpose of being a spearhead in the heart of the Muslim world."

During the conference, Mohammed Salah—the Chicago-based Hamas commander—organized a series of smaller workshops for Hidmi and other recruits at a nearby Ramada Inn. At the front of the room, a burly man introduced himself as Ibrahim Mahmoud Muzayyin, director of an organization now called the Holy Land Foundation for Relief and Development (at the time called the Occupied Land Fund), which officially raises money for charity in the West Bank and Gaza. According to the information retrieved by Israeli investigators, Muzayyin told the group: "You have been assembled here because you are all residents of the occupied territories. And you have been chosen to carry out operations to escalate the intifadah on behalf of the Hamas movement." After a series of pep talks, the group broke into smaller clusters. The instructor explained that everyone would undergo instruction in handling improvised explosives and hand grenades and in building car bombs. They would also receive training in subjects such as interrogation and execution of collaborators, surveillance and political organizing.

Six months later, the group met again in Kansas City. This time, Mohammed Salah introduced Najib al-Ghosh, now the editor of MAYA's flagship magazine. Al-Ghosh lectured on the interrogation methods used by Israeli intelligence, as well as on different kinds of hand grenades and bombs. According to Israeli information, Salah interjected, "The purpose of all this is so that everyone will go home and plant explosives in the area where he lives."

Upon his return to Israel, Hidmi was arrested. In early 1993, Salah, too, was arrested by Israeli authorities and indicted in the Ramallah Military Court. When news of his detainment was first reported in the U.S., along with Israeli complaints that Hamas had established a terror network here, the FBI initially dismissed the allegations. "We were wrong," says former FBI official Revell. "We didn't know what was going on in our own backyard." During Salah's interrogation, conducted in Arabic, he confessed—albeit by signing a Hebrew document—to making several surreptitious trips to Israel, where he directed Hamas operations and transferred $230,000 for the purchase of weapons out of a total of $790,000 he intended to bring later. He revealed that in Chicago he kept a map of where two kidnapped executed Israeli soldiers were buried by Hamas death squads. And he told of how, following the deportation of the Hamas leadership to Lebanon, he helped rebuild the group's command structure. Other information obtained by Israeli authorities confirmed that, since 1987, Salah had recruited hundreds of Hamas operatives, arranged for their training in car bombs and other explosive devices (including chemical weapons) and even built fourteen timers for explosives himself.

Hamas has been the most successful of the militant Islamic organizations both in sending its officials to work in U.S.-based organizations and in raising funds here. Today, law enforcement and intelligence officials say, the most senior-ranking Hamas official living in the United States is Sheik Jamal Said of the Bridgeview Mosque in Chicago. Although Said has denied any links to Hamas, Salah and other Hamas operatives have told Israeli intelligence that they received instructions from him. U.S. officials also maintain that Said has worked closely with and on behalf of two other groups with ties to Hamas: the Islamic Association for Palestine (IAP) and the Holy Land Foundation for Relief and Development.Both groups are headquartered in Richardson, Texas, less than a mile apart, in nondescript strip shopping malls. "There's no doubt," says Revell, that these two groups are Hamas fronts."

What are these organizations? The Holy Land Foundation is Hamas's overt fund-raising arm in the United States. According to its English brochures, it openly solicits tax-deductible donations for such charitable causes as "needy Palestinian children, health clinics and schools." While some of its money is spent accordingly, most of its funds are routed though local Zakat (or mandatory Islamic charity tax) organizations run by Hamas in the West Bank and Gaza. These organizations not only serve to indoctrinate Muslim youths into radical Islamist ideology, but also provide covert cash conduits to Hamas military squads.

The IAP, while claiming that it conducts no fund-raising for activities outside the United States, does operate an extensive propagandanetwork, according to a review of internal materials, videos and documents. Indeed, with offices and affiliates in more than a dozen cities, IAP is a veritable public relations machine. It publishes newspapers, produces terrorist training and recruitment videos (some showing terrorists who boast of their "kills" and interrogations of "collaborators" just before their executions), disseminates videos, organizes conferences and even sponsors a traveling Hamas musical troupe. (One of the troupe's songs includes the refrain: "We buy Paradise with the blood of the Jews.")

The IAP also publishes the largest Arabic-language newspaper in the United States, *al-Zaitonah*, as well as the English-language *Muslim World Monitor*. Both papers frequently celebrate successful Hamas terrorist attacks. An October 1994 headline in *al-Zaitonah*, for example, proclaimed, "In Its Greatest Operation, Hamas Takes Credit for the Bombing of an Israeli Bus in the Center of Tel Aviv." Other articles warn of anti-Muslim conspiracies, such as an alleged joint plot by the Mossad and the FBI to bomb the World Trade Center and throw the blame on Muslims. Despite such incendiary content, however, ATT, MCI and other companies, as well as the U.S. Bureau of Prisons (which is in search of Muslim chaplains) have advertised in IAP publications.

Although IAP officials assure American reporters that their organization is not hostile to the United States, its conferences and publications tell a different story. In August 1990, for example, it organized an emergency conference of leading Hamas figures (recorded by IAP itself on both video and audio tape) in response to the U.S. troop buildup in Saudi Arabia. The participants issued a resolution condemning "the American crusades." Some, like Khalil al-Qawka, a Hamas leader from Palestine, wanted to go further, as he said in an address to the group: "Today, America is right here at your doorstep, in everybody's house. Ba'al, the idol, is back and stands erect in the Arabian peninsula. Is there a Muhammad to slay the Ba'al of our times?... The Marines, dear brothers, are stealing the doors of your houses, and the doors of your mosques, in obstinate and open provocation. They are at our doors. Their plan is to penetrate the flesh of our girls. And our honor, and our values, in order to turn our society into a perverted nation." Later, a choir of 8- and 9-year-old children sang revolutionary Islamist songs praising the Intifadah and Hamas.

On a narrow, dead-end street in Tampa, Florida, a sign is affixed to the last house on the block. "Izz al-Din al-Qassam...declared Jihad against the British and Zionist invasion of Palestine," it reads. "He was martyred on November 19, 1935, in Ya'bad, Palestine. Al-Qassam has become a symbol of heroism, resistance, occupation and invasion of steadfast Palestine." Indeed, for militant Palestinians, al-Qassam may be the most exalted figure in recent history. As noted by the Palestinian scholar Ziad Abu-Amr, al-Qassam is "the main source of inspiration for the Islamic Jihad movement.... He is viewed...as the true father of the armed Islamic Revolution."

In Gaza, there is another mosque with the same name. It's a hangout for the Palestine Islamic Jihad, a group known for decapitating and dismembering Jews and Palestinian "collaborators" and for its suicide bombings in Israel. The Jihad sees Israel's existence as part of a larger, American-directed plot against Islam, which explains why it might find it useful to maintain offshoots of some kind in the United States. According to Ziad Abu-Amr, "The Islamic Jihad movement sees Israel and America as two faces of the same coin."

Operating out of the al-Qassam Mosque on 130th Street is a group officially called the Islamic Committee for Palestine, a subsidiary, in turn, of the Islamic Concern Project. The latter defines itself as a "charitable, cultural, social, educational and religious [group] in which the concept of brotherhood, freedom, justice, unity, piety, righteousness and peace shall be propagated." It also functions as a support group to the Islamic Jihad in the U.S.

The Islamic Committee is headed by the soft-spoken Sami al-Arian, a professor of engineering at the University of South Florida. In an interview, al-Arian denied any connection to Islamic Jihad and claimed that his organization was not "political" but rather a "charitable, social and cultural-type group." When I asked him who al-Qassam was, he shrugged, "Oh, he was just a scholar." Al-Arian's claims notwithstanding, the bank account used by the Islamic Committee, according to knowledgeable sources, has been used to transfer money to and from Islamic Jihad "charities." Islamic Jihad's international Arabic newsletter (published until 1991 under the name *Islam and Palestine*) and an occasional venue for Islamic Jihad communiques taking credit for terrorist attacks, listed the main address on its masthead as the Islamic Committee's post office box in Tampa.

When I asked al-Arian whether *Islam and Palestine* had any connection to the Islamic Jihad, he said, "I've seen most of the issues. I never saw the word Jihad on it." But a review of past issues shows that the journal has often glorified Jihad. An editorial in the December 1991 issue stated, for example, "We support with full force the call of the honorable [Ayatollah] Ali Khamenei to the Ummah for Jihad to banish the Great Satan."

One of the Islamic Committee's accessory institutions is the World and Islam Studies Enterprise (WISE), also in Tampa, which functions ostensibly as an Islamist academic outreach center, inviting out-of-town Middle East scholars and analysts to deliver lectures. Two years ago, it sponsored the visit of Hassan al-Turabi, the de facto leader of the Sudan, a terrorism-sponsoring country whose diplomats were involved in the second set of attempted bombings in the World Trade Center conspiracy. (While in Tampa, al-Turabi stayed in Sami al-Arian'shome.) Last year, WISE invited Rachid al-Ghannouchi, head of the militant Tunisian fundamentalist group, to speak, but the State Department refused to grant him a visa after evidence was submitted demonstrating his support for terrorism. WISE has since established a formal affiliation with the University of South Florida.

One of the more unusual visitors to Tampa over the past several years has been Sheik Abdul Aziz Odeh, the spiritual leader of the Palestine Islamic Jihad. Following his deportation from Gaza in 1988, Odeh quickly set up offices and branches in Beirut, Amman and Damascus. Odeh later entered the U.S., slipping past INS officials unaware of his role political identity and later gravitating to two cities in particular: Brooklyn, where he had become a hero to El-Sayyid Nosair and other militants; and Tampa. In Brooklyn, Odeh became so actively involved with the World Trade Center conspiracy defendants that he was named as the only unindicted co-conspirator in the Trade Center bombing.

"...the Islamic Committee's annual conferences have been instrumental in bridging traditional divisions between radical Shiites and Sunnis."

Although al-Arian and the Islamic Committee have assumed a relatively low profile in Tampa, the Islamic Committee's annual conferences have been instrumental in bridging traditional divisions between radical Shiites and Sunnis. Held in St. Louis and Chicago from 1989 through 1992, the Islamic Committee's annual conferences have consistently featured incendiary calls by radical Islamists—including Abdul Rahman and Rachid al-Ghannouchi—to attack Jewish and Western targets. One year, al-Arian himself opened up the conference with this preamble: "We assemble today to stand up and pay our respects to the march of the martyrs, which increases and does not decrease, and to the river of blood that gushes forth and does not extinguish. From butchery to butchery and from martyrdom to martyrdom, from Jihad to Jihad."

Asked about Abdul Rahman's presence at the conference, al-Arian became defensive, insisting that the sheik "was not invited," that he "just dropped in" and was only allowed to address the "youth and children."The Islamic Committee's own publication, however, says that the sheik shared the podium with Palestine Islamic Jihad's head Abdul Azziz Odeh in a panel discussion titled "Insights into the Islamic March in Resistance and Victory."

In the past eighteen months, some of Abdul Rahman's apparatus has decamped from the East Coast and moved to new headquarters in San Diego, California. The San Diego-based American Islamic Group, for example, a self-described "humanitarian Islamic organization," maintains contact with and raises money for Algeria's Armed Islamic Group, the Philippines's Abu Sayyaf terrorist splinter organization, the Palestinian Hamas and Islamic Jihad and, above all, Sheik Umar's own al-Gama'a al-Islamiyah of Egypt. Its bilingual newsletter, the *Islam Report*, calls on Muslims to support these militant causes. A typical piece in one issue, dealing with the "execution" of an Egyptian officer by al-Gama'a guerrillas, asserts: "The Mujahideen have carried out the judgment of Allah." A report on an American Air Force accident, in which sixteen Americans were killed, has the headline: "O Allah, Lock Their Throats in Their Own Traps!"

Kifah al-Jayousi, the director of the American Islamic Group, is one of Sheik Umar's many Palestinian followers. Among other achievements, he has pioneered Islamist activity on the Internet, transmitting militant messages and requests for funds (despite Internet regulations that forbid fund-raising). "My network is vast, and I have branches all over the United States," al-Jayousi told a caller posing as a potential donor over the phone. "I keep closely in touch with Mujahideen in most Muslim countries, too."

Within the American Muslim population of 5 to 6 million, radical groups and their adherents represent only an extremist fringe.Their militant interpretation of Islam does not reflect mainstream Islam, which eschews violence and thoroughly repudiates terrorism. But Muslimorganizations are increasingly succumbing to the influence of militant Islam. "Islamic fundamentalists now control many of the Muslim organizations in the United States," says journalist Ahmed Said Nasr. As a result, Nasr says, "there is more genuine intellectual freedom of expression for Muslims living in Cairo than in the United States."

Even groups that represent themselves as mainstream, such as the Washington-based Council on American Islamic Relations (which is partly funded, according to a confidential source with knowledge of CAIR's finances, by radical Persian Gulf donors) attempt to legitimize militant Islam by attacking all criticism of it as racist. Giving the council "a platform to claim they are protecting Muslim civil rights," says Ashmawi, "is like giving David Duke a platform to claim he is a civil libertarian." While the council presents itself as a group concerned with fair treatment for Muslims, its media campaigns intentionally obscure the distinction between the overwhelming majority of peaceful, law-abiding Muslims and the radical militant minority.

The cruel irony for the vast majority of Muslim immigrants who came to the U.S. to escape Islamist turmoil in their homelands is that the proliferation of radical Islamist groups on American soil throws them back into the old vortex of polarized politics many had sought to escape. The danger is another matter. Militant Islam remains a fringe element in Western Muslim communities. But, as the World Trade Center bombing shows, it does not take a big group to make a big catastrophe.

Militia Movement: Prescription for Disaster[3]

Extremists, particularly those engaged in paramilitary training, present a serious danger. They hate the government, believe there are Federal conspiracies, and are convinced an armed showdown is coming.

The militia movement came under intense national scrutiny after the April 19, 1995, bombing of the Federal Building in Oklahoma City, when it was reported that two suspects, Timothy McVeigh and Terry Nichols, had attended militia meetings in Michigan. In addition, prosecutors charged that McVeigh was motivated out of anger at the Federal government for its handling of the Branch Davidian confrontation in Waco, Tex.—an issue that has been one of the chief rallying cries of the militia movement.

There is evidence that the militia movement has continued to grow since the Oklahoma City bombing. The pattern is not uniform, but militia gains plainly appear to outweigh losses—contrary to the widespread expectation that public shock and revulsion at the bombing might prompt the militias to disband. Many hard-core militiamen believe that the U.S. government itself committed the bombing to create an excuse for further depriving citizens of their constitutional rights.

A survey by the Anti-Defamation League reveals that the militia movement has spread, with some of the growth taking place after the Oklahoma City bombing. Militias have been found to be operating in at least 40 states, with membership reaching about 15,000. While these findings are not a definitive indication of the militias' future prospects,they do point to the need for ongoing close attention to this movement.

Since the militias mainly are located in rural and small-town communities, the burden of monitoring them falls largely on state and local law enforcement agencies. Many of these agencies—in large measure for lack of adequate investigative resources—have not yet managed to rise to this task. That job will be made even more difficult if, as some militias' strategists are counseling, the groups adopt a strategy of organizing into small units designed to be less susceptible to detection, monitoring, and infiltration by law enforcement agencies. This approach echoes a strategic concept known as "leaderless resistance" that has been promoted in recent years by several far-right figures, including Tom Metzger, who leads the White Aryan Resistance, and Louis Beam, a former Texas Ku Klux Klan Grand Dragon, who has been "Ambassador-At-Large" of the Idaho-based Aryan Nations.

"Militias have been found to be operating in at least 40 states..."

[3]Article by Thomas Halpern, acting director, Fact Finding Department; David Rosenberg, assistant director, Fact Finding Department; and Irwin Suall, director of special projects, Anti-Defamation League, NY, from *USA Today Magazine* 124:16 Ja 1, '96. Copyright © 1996 by Society for the Advancement of Education. Reprinted with permission.

The most ominous aspect of the militias' program is the conviction, openly expressed by many of them, that an impending armed conflict with the Federal government necessitates paramilitary training and the stockpiling of weapons in preparation for that day of reckoning. According to the militias' conspiracy view, the Federal authorities are enacting gun control legislation in order to make it impossible for the people to resist the imposition of a tyrannical regime or a "one-world" dictatorship. Many militia supporters believe that the conspiracy involves not only Federal authorities, but the United Nations, foreign troops, and other "sinister" forces. Some militia propaganda continues to exhibit an anti-Semitic strain that well could become more pervasive as a result of the movement's obsessive conspiracy-mongering.

"Some militia firebrands reach their audience through mail-order videotapes, computer bulletin boards, and the Internet."

In this connection, the role of America's leading anti-Semitic organization, Liberty Lobby, and its weekly publication, *The Spotlight*, merit attention. Many of the conspiracy fantasies fueling the militias were promoted heavily in a September, 1994, eight-page supplement of *The Spotlight*, which posed the questions: "Is America on the verge of war? Is a 'national emergency' about to be declared and America placed under martial law? Is America on the brink of occupation by military troops under United Nations control?" In addition, the Militia of Montana has been promoting for sale in its catalogue a comprehensive bomb-making manual entitled *The Road Back*, produced by Liberty Lobby's publishing arm, Noontide Press. The catalogue describes the book as "a plan for the restoration of freedom when our country has been taken over by its enemies."

The militia movement's continued expansion is due at least partly to an effective communications network. Organizers have promoted their ideology not only at militia meetings, but at gun shows, "patriot" rallies, and gatherings of various groups with anti-government grievances. Some militia firebrands reach their audience through mail-order videotapes, computer bulletin boards, and the Internet. Exploiting yet another medium, the pro-militia American Patriot Fax Network disseminates material from hate-group spokesmen and conspiracy theorists, including some who proclaim that the government orchestrated the Oklahoma City bombing.

Of course, the fact that the men charged with the Oklahoma City bombing have had some association with one militia group does not make the entire movement responsible for the crime. Even if no further connection is established between the bombing and the militias, though, it should be clear by now that these extremists, particularly those engaged in paramilitary training, present a serious danger. The formula they have concocted—belief in Federal conspiracies, hatred of the government, and the conviction that an armed showdown is coming—is a prescription for disaster. The following is a state-by-state summary of militia activity:

Alabama has a small, but steadily growing, militia movement. Its most active groups, which appear to be in regular contact with one another, are the Gadsden Minutemen of Etowah County and the Montgomery County-based Sons of Liberty. The Gadsden

Minutemen regularly publish a newsletter and meet periodically to practice battle skills and hand-to-hand combat techniques.

The Sons of Liberty is a small group with a deliberately low profile. The organization's manual advises members to "keep the group size down. If you've got more than 10-12 spin off another group." Followers also are warned not to "keep all your eggs in one basket. If you have more than one rifle, keep it in a hideaway spot." Finally, the handbook counsels, "Don't lose sight of our objective.... Don't fire unless fired upon, but if they [Federal officials] mean to have a war let it begin here."

Alaska. Small militias have formed in the state. Despite their modest size, the groups have caused concern among observers. An Anchorage attorney and board member of the National Rifle Association has called some of the militias "extremely dangerous." Alaskan militias are connected to the national militia movement via computers. The electronic bulletin board services "AmeriKa" and "Back Woods," based in Anchorage, provide users with conspiracy literature and act as forums to lambast the purportedly encroaching powers of the Federal government.

Arizona. William Cooper of St. Johns has broadcast a nightly shortwave radio program, "Hour of the Time," promoting militias and "New World Order" conspiracy theories. Jack McLamb, a former Phoenix policeman and founder of Police Against the New World Order, aims to convince law enforcement officials of a plot to create a one-world government through his conspiracy tract, *Operation Vampire Killer 2000*, and a newsletter, *Aid & Abet*. Another lawman, Graham County Sheriff Richard Mack, has spoken at gatherings about his successful suit against the U.S. government to avoid enforcement of the Brady Law in his county, an action that has earned him the admiration of militiamen nationwide.

Militia organizing in the state has occurred in the areas of Phoenix, Prescott, Payson, Snowflake, Kingman, Pinedale, and the Four Comers, with continued expansion since the Oklahoma City bombing. In April, 1995, two men from Snowflake with reported ties to a militia were charged with illegal conspiracy to manufacture, possess, and sell 20 grenades to a Federal undercover agent. They reportedly said that their group was arming itself for a confrontation with the Federal government.

Arkansas. Militia organizing remains embryonic, with one to three groups in the northwest region of the state. They are not known to engage in paramilitary training.

California's militia movement has been growing rapidly, with approximately 35 units throughout the state. The locations range from urban centers to small towns, and extend from the northern to southern borders. Counties in which militias have been active include Los Angeles, Orange, San Bernardino, San Diego, Kern, Placer, Alameda, Marin, Santa Clara, Shasta, San Joaquin, Stanislaus, El Dorado, Tulare, Sonoma, Mendocino, Butte, Tuolumne, and Tehama.

This widespread activity has been encouraged on public access television and radio. "The Informed Citizen," a television program broadcast on Redding's public access channel, Michael Zwerling's radio talk show on KSCO in Santa Cruz, and "Truth Radio" KDNO in Delano all promote militias.

Dean Compton of rural Shasta County has founded the National Alliance of Christian Militias in response to the perceived threat of an impending "New World Order." The group, whose members are armed, reportedly blends biblical teachings and survivalism. Training sessions are conducted on Compton's 130-acre ranch.

Activist-recruiter Mark Koernke has spoken around the state. In Concord, he reportedly described a future takeover of the U.S. by foreign "New World Order" troops and claimed that the Federal Emergency Management Agency (FEMA) will establish concentration camps for American citizens." The solution," he claimed, "is militias. It looks like we're going to pull the trigger. We eventually will. No doubt about that." In May, 1995, he addressed a "Taking America Back" conference in Palm Springs. The organizer of the event, Tom Johns, claims to be the "intelligence officer" for the Morongo Valley Militia.

Colorado. Sources indicate that militia organizing has been frozen in the aftermath of the Oklahoma City bombing. Meetings have been put on hold, though it does not appear that the groups have disbanded. Nevertheless, anti-Federal government and conspiracy-oriented tirades continue to be phoned in by listeners to radio station KHNC in Johnstown, which broadcasts a steady stream of "patriot" programs. Some callers have expressed the view, held by many militia supporters, that the government itself carried out the Oklahoma City blast. Another important vehicle for pro-militia activism in Colorado is *The USA Patriot Magazine*, published monthly by the USA Patriot Network in Johnstown. The periodical, whose cover price is "4 FRNs" (Federal Reserve Notes), contains a "Telephone Address Book" listing dozens of contacts.

Colorado's militia movement has been defended publicly by State Sen. Charles Duke, who has said that "the few militia people I know practice a policy of nonviolence...not altogether too different from a Boy Scout kind of idea." Following the Oklahoma City bombing, a *Denver Post* columnist reported that Duke raised the possibility of a government role in the bombing: "They're certainly capable of it. Look what they did to Waco. There's many people around the country who believe they did it.... Is it unreasonable to see the continuation of a pattern here?"

Delaware. The Delaware Regional Citizens Militia, located in the central part of the state, began organizing in the early months of 1995. Leader Andrew Brown has claimed that membership in the group is so secretive he would identify "only seven or so, even if you tortured me."

Florida. Militias and their "patriot" supporters are operating in the following counties: Alachua, Duval, Clay, St. Johns, Marion, Orange,Brevard, Highlands, St. Lucie, Martin, Volusia, Indian River, Okeechobee, Pinellas, Sarasota, Pasco, Polk, Hillsborough, Palm

Beach, and Monroe. On Dec. 3, 1994, outside Melbourne, a collection of anti-government activists and militia groups organized a "Patriot Alert Rally." Martin "Red" Beckman, a tax protestor from Montana, told the gathering, "They lied to us about Pearl Harbor and Vietnam and Korea and the energy crisis and the Kennedy assassination. We don't want to have to go to the militia if we can help it. But if we don't have truth in this country, part of the judgment that's going to come on this country is going to come from the militia."

For sale at the rally were copies of *The New Federalist* (a publication of political extremist Lyndon LaRouche); *The Spotlight*; literature from the St. Lucie-based Florida State Militia, 2nd Regiment; and a handbill from the Brevard County Militia proclaiming: "Wake-up America, Your country is being taken over bit-by-bit. Join Your fellow PATRIOTS to STOP this MOVEMENT."

In Pensacola, militias are promoted by Chuck Baldwin, the pastor of Crossroads Baptist Church, who hosts a radio show on the Christian Patriot Network and invites listeners to call in: "We're talking about citizens' militias, Federal government's encroachment on individual rights, New World Order, United Nations, gun control, it's all related." Militias also are promoted on the public access channel in Alachua County that airs a pro-militia video produced by the North Florida Patriot Association.

Georgia. Frank Smith, an Air Force veteran and retired tool-and-die maker, claims to lead the Georgia Militia. Days after the Oklahoma City bombing, Smith echoed the sentiments of militia leaders across thecountry by blaming the U.S. government for the blast. Speaking on the CNN television program "Talkback Live," Smith said the government was "trying to get the militia movement to come out and fight. We expected them to do something drastic. We didn't expect it to be that drastic."

Rick Tyler of Epworth directs a so-called constitutionalist, anti-tax group known as the Georgia Taxpayers Association and co-hosts "Voice of Liberty," a daily shortwave radio program. Soon after the Oklahoma City bombing, "Voice of Liberty" listeners were told that the disaster was being used by the government as an excuse "to put across their agenda of establishing a police state.... They are ruthless; they are cunning; they are cutthroat; and furthermore, we are their target."

Another organization, known as Citizens for a Constitutional Georgia, meets weekly at an Atlanta hotel. Materials available for sale at the meetings have included pro-gun literature, The Protocols of the *Elders of Zion*, and *The Spotlight*. The groups has sponsored local appearances by militia activists. Moreover, a militia group in north Georgia conducts paramilitary maneuvers on a 38-acre tract in Hall County, northeast of Atlanta.

Idaho's militia movement has attempted to achieve mainstream acceptance. Carefully toning down his group's rhetoric, militia leader Samuel Sherwood, of the Blackfoot-based United States Militia Association, has told Idaho lawmakers that his organization is working for change within the political system. On other occasions, however, he has derided the state's government and has seemed to encourage violence against its representatives.

In March, 1995, after meeting with Idaho Lt. Gov. Butch Otter, Sherwood complained that some Idaho politicians ignored the interests of state citizens in favor of a Federal agenda. His advice to followers was: "Go up and look legislators in the face, because some day you may have to blow it off."

Former Green Beret James "Bo" Gritz, who is building a survivalist community in central Idaho, has engaged in activities that closely have paralleled those of the militia movement. He has traveled the country conducting a weapons and survival training course he calls SPIKE—Specially Prepared Individuals for Key Events—and has called for the execution as traitors of the "tyrants" responsible for the government's actions in the standoff with white supremacist Randy Weaver in Idaho and the Branch Davidian conflagration at Waco. Gritz deplored the Oklahoma City bombing, yet praised its technique. At a speech in Dallas, he labeled the blast a "Rembrandt," and said he considered it a "masterpiece of science and art put together."

Illinois. A Lombard-based organization called the Illinois Minutemen describes itself as a militia and has echoed the anti-government themes of militia groups elsewhere. The group claims members from Cook, DuPage, Will, Kane, and McHenry counties. It meets twice a month at a Lombard bowling alley. Members do not wear uniforms or carry weapons, but reportedly are considering a paramilitary training session with the Michigan Militia.

Another organization, the Southern Illinois Patriots League, held a rally on April 22, 1995, in Carbondale to protest the presentation by Gov. James Edgar of the state's highest honor, the Order of Lincoln, to gun control advocate James Brady. Signs at the rally, which drew 150 participants, described James Brady and his wife Sarah as "diabolical misfits" and equated agents of the U.S. Bureau of Alcohol, Tobacco and Firearms with Nazi storm troopers. Protestors were invited to wipe their feet on a United Nations Flag.

Indiana. Militias have become active across the state in St. Joseph's, Allen, Johnson, Marion, Ripley, Warrick, and Dearborn counties. Many of the groups are part of the larger Indiana Citizens Volunteer Militia, a state-wide umbrella organization that coordinates militia activities.

Linda Thompson of Indianapolis operates a computer bulletin board for militia groups across the country. She has announced to prospective new members that her bulletin board is for "doers, not whiners or talkers." She explained that potential members had to be willing to provide the movement with substantial assistance, such as a training site, ammunition, skills training, food, medical care, or money. On May 12, 1995, Thompson was arrested by Marion County police and charged with resisting arrest and disorderly conduct; the case is pending. According to officials, she carried a concealed weapon into the county prosecutor's office and refused to show her permit for the gun.

The Boonville-based North American Volunteer Militia is directed by Joe Holland, who describes himself as a patriotic "freedom fighter." He reportedly is under investigation by Federal authorities for bank, bankruptcy, and securities fraud and tax evasion. In April, 1995, Holland urged followers to travel to Ravalli County, Mont., to show their support for militia members there who had engaged in an armed confrontation with police. He surrendered to Indiana authorities after being charged in Montana with criminal syndicalism.

James Heath, a member of the Indianapolis Police Department, heads the Johnson County Militia. In May, 1995, speaking before a Greenwood-based group called the Sovereign Patriots, he derisively referred to Indianapolis Mayor Stephen Goldsmith as "Goldstein." Noting that the mayor's home address is unlisted, Heath also asserted that Goldsmith had something to hide. In a subsequent apology, Heath employed an anti-Semitic stereotype to argue that his slur was really a compliment. Several days later, Indianapolis Police Department officials disciplined Heath for his remarks by demoting him from sergeant to patrolman.

Iowa. Militia groups have formed, but there is little evidence of their size and influence. Paul Stauffer, an Air Force veteran living in Cedar Rapids and the self-described "national contact" for the Iowa Militia, has claimed that his organization operates in 35 counties, but has not offered specific membership figures. He contends that militia members are concerned with "intelligence" gathering activities, and that the group maintains contacts with militia leaders across the country.

Kansas. C.D. Olsen of Lyndon leads the Kansas Citizens Militia (also known as the Kansas Unorganized Citizens Militia). Olsen took over from Morris E. Wilson, previously the group's commander and now its executive officer. Wilson claims militia units are organizing in Wichita, Junction City, and Topeka, where at one meeting he played host to Michigan militia proponent Mark Koernke.

Kentucky. There are two relatively small militia groups. Danny and Diane Snellon are, respectively, the coordinator and secretary/treasurer of the Kentucky Citizens Militia. Meetings have taken place at the main branch of the Lexington Public Library and at a sportsman's shop in Paris, northeast of Lexington. Attendance at these meetings has ranged from 10 to 20 people.

In Boone County, a militia called the Defenders of Liberty is believed to have a core group of 30 to 40 individuals. Unlike the Kentucky Citizens Militia, the Defenders of Liberty wear uniforms and undergo paramilitary training.

Louisiana. In Lafayette, the Militia of Louisiana has engaged in paramilitary and urban combat training, and is thought to number about 55 members—some of whom have had affiliations with so-called constitutionalist groups.

Michigan. The Northern Michigan Regional Militia, also known as the Michigan Militia, attracted national attention in the wake of the April 19 bombing of the Federal Building in Oklahoma City.

Group leaders have said that Terry Nichols, a suspect in the Oklahoma blast, attended several of its meetings and that on at least one occasion brought another suspect, Timothy McVeigh. Federal agents searching the farm of Terry Nichols' brother James uncovered a number of documents relating to the Michigan Militia.

Leaders of the Michigan Militia have disagreed with Federal officials about the identity of the bomber and have offered a theory of their own. A week after the blast, commander Norman Olson and his chief of staff, Ray Southwell, announced that they believed the Japanese had bombed the Oklahoma building in retaliation for the nerve gas attack on the Tokyo subways. Olson and Southwell said that act was engineered by the American government. When their view was repudiated by a majority of the Militia's board, the two men immediately resigned from their positions. Olson assured the press that, nevertheless, "the Michigan Militia is as strong as ever," and that he and Southwell will remain members of the organization.

Minutes after the bombing, activist Mark Koernke (AKA "Mark from Michigan"), whose militant "how-to" videotapes have made him a prime recruiter for the movement, faxed a cryptic, handwritten message about the bombing to Rep. Steve Stockman (R.-Tex.). "First update," the fax read in part. "Seven to 10 floors only. Military people on the scene." Koernke insisted he had no prior knowledge of the bombing, and that he had only sent the fax hoping Stockman would "get cameras in place as soon as possible."

Koernke has been identified as spokesman of the Michigan Militia-at-Large, characterized as a more radical offshoot of the Michigan Militia. He has promoted conspiracy theories to audiences around the country, including several in the Pacific Northwest while on a speaking tour sponsored by the Militia of Montana.

Until recently, Koernke also hosted "The Intelligence Report," a shortwave radio program that aired five times a week. Days after the Oklahoma bombing, Koernke told listeners that Federal agents had outfitted suspect Timothy McVeigh in a bright orange jumpsuit in order to make him an easy assassination target. Koernke's program subsequently was pulled from the airwaves by WWCR, the Nashville, Tenn., shortwave radio station that had been broadcasting his daily diatribes to 2,700,000 listeners in the U.S. and a number of foreign countries. "We've got to get the gasoline off the fires," insisted the station manager.

Minnesota. There are several small militia groups sprinkled across the state, including the Arrowhead Regional Militia in Duluth, the St. Cloud-based Metro Militia, and the Red Pine Regional Militia, located in the Minneapolis area.

Mississippi. Drew Rayner of Ocean Springs has spearheaded recruitment for the Mississippi Militia. On April 28, 1995, he appeared before a group of about 75 near Laurel. Literature available at the meeting included the Mississippi Militia "Information

Booklet," which contained a 20-page manual on the formation of a militia; *The Revolutionary Spirit*, a tabloid that excerpted material from Liberty Lobby's *The Spotlight*; and *Operation Vampire Killer 2000*, a manual by former Phoenix, Ariz., policeman Jack McLamb that aims to convince law enforcement officials of a one-world government conspiracy.

Missouri. The Buckner-based Missouri Patriots' newsletter, *The Militia Minute*, rails against the Federal government, "international bankers," and the media. While its size is not known, leaders of the militia also are members of the Kansas City-based White Knights of the Ku Klux Klan. In addition, a promotional item for the White Knights in their publication, *The White Beret*, features the slogan: "Join the White Militia."

Statewide, militias have been established in an estimated 14 counties and are recruiting actively. Although they maintain separate identities, several units in the eastern section of Missouri appear to operate under the leadership of the St. Louis-based 1st Missouri Volunteers Militia. Groups in the western part of the state are directed by the Missouri 51st Militia of Kansas City. The Springfield-area 24th Missouri Militia is the largest and most influential such group in the southeastern part of the state.

In March, 1995, the 1st Missouri Volunteers assembled a gathering of six state militia groups for a Missouri Regional Conference. Speakers, including State Sen. David Klarich, declared that, unlike their counter-parts in other states, the Missouri Militia does not promote an agenda of bigotry. However, literature offered at the meeting included extracts from hate publications like *The Spotlight*; *The Truth at Last*, published by anti-Jewish agitator Ed Fields of Georgia; and *The Jubilee*, a journal that espouses the anti-Semitic pseudo-theology of the "Identity Church" movement.

Montana's militia groups, whose armed members have been embroiled in hostile confrontations with police, are among the most volatile in the country. The Militia of Montana (MOM), one of the movement's most visible and extreme groups, has continued to spread its message around Montana and the nation from its headquarters in the small town of Noxon. MOM was founded by John Trochmann—who has been a speaker at a major conclave of the white supremacist Aryan Nations.

An item in an issue of MOM's monthly newsletter, *Taking Aim*, printed several weeks before the bombing of the Oklahoma City Federal Building, underscores the centrality of the date, April 19, to the group's ideology. The newsletter noted April 19, 1995, as the upcoming execution date ("UNLESS WE ACT NOW!!!," it read) for convicted murderer and white supremacist Richard Wayne Snell. The item recounted that April 19 was also the day on which "Lexington burned.... Warsaw burned.... The feds attempted to raid Randy Weaver.... The Branch Davidians burned." By citing Lexington and Warsaw, MOM seems to compare the U.S. government to colonial America's British rulers and to the genocidal Nazi regime, while simultaneously agitating on behalf of a racist and anti-Semitic killer.

As in the case with many militia groups around the country, its leaders are obsessed with the notion that UN troops, aided by Soviet-made weapons, are planning a takeover of the U.S. An "Intelligence Report" distributed by MOM purports to provide followers with detailed documentation of this conspiracy. A National Guard base in Biloxi, Miss., is said to be filled with tracks "of Soviet origin," whose "fuel tanks have been topped off and apparently look ready to roll." The report adds: "These tracks are being marked at this time United Nations."

The Militia on Montana distributes a catalogue that offers for sale numerous videotapes, audiotapes, and publications on a variety of conspiracy themes, as well as a comprehensive bomb-making and warfare manual, *The Road Back*—"A plan for the restoration of freedom when our country has been taken over by its enemies, 20 chapters on organization, recruiting, intelligence, communications, supply, weapons, sabotage, medicine, warfare, and training, etc."

Nebraska. An Omaha-based militia that has used several names, including the Constitutional Reinstatement Group and the Nebraska Militia, meets bi-weekly. At these meetings, the anti-Jewish screed *The Protocols of the Elders of Zion* has been offered for sale. The group does not appear to engage in paramilitary training.

New Hampshire. The Hillsborough Troop of Dragoons' leader, Fitzhugh MacCrae, told *The Boston Globe* that his group comprises 63 members, of whom two-thirds are allegedly combat veterans. While he emphasizes the group's benign and civic activities, he also boasts, "We're probably better armed than the Army."

The White Mountain Militia operates in Cornish under the leadership of N. Scott Stevens, who describes himself as director of the militia's "Information Services." Stevens hosted a May 14, 1995, rally in the Cornish town hall for militia members, extreme anti-gun control groups, and others hostile to the Federal government.

New Mexico. Militias operate in counties around Albuquerque and Santa Fe and in the northwestern area of the state. On Oct. 22, 1994, six militia organizations from these regions met in Raton in an unsuccessful attempt to form a combined New Mexico militia. Gov. Gary Johnson was criticized for meeting with militia representatives on April 28, 1995, although he claimed that he did so in order to ensure that they remain non-violent. A Farmington militia is known to promote neo-Nazi and white supremacist sentiments.

New York. Several groups are clustered along the New York-Pennsylvania line. Established militias include the Citizens Militia, Chemung Division, founded in Chemung County in November, 1994, which engages in paramilitary training and receives literature from the Militia of Montana and militia groups in Michigan, providing further confirmation that groups in those two states serve as important propaganda sources for militias around the country.

Militias also have organized in Tioga, Steuben, Schuyler, Chenango, Cortland, and Broome counties. In Chenango County, militiaman Francis Catlin, who uses the code name "Moonshiner," has said that outrage over the Waco conflagration fueled the militia movement in upstate New York. "We figure this country is in real bad shape," he has commented, adding that "Jewish people" are responsible for the financial difficulties faced by grain farmers.

Near New York City, militias were formed in November, 1994, in Dutchess and Orange counties. The Orange County Militia, also known as the Committee of Correspondence, has distributed literature incorporating conspiracy theories from political extremist Lyndon LaRouche. Founder Walter Reddy, while reportedly distancing himself from the group, expressed the suspicion that the Federal government was involved in the Oklahoma City bombing. Reddy stated, "It was CIA-orchestrated, from the information I have."

North Carolina. The Alamance Minutemen is a small and secretive militia group whose communications appear to be conducted largely through the "Spirit of '76" computer bulletin board, operated by the group's leader, Jeff Rudd of Alamance County. Another organization, Citizens for the Reinstatement of Constitutional Government, meets in the towns of Monroe and Matthews, both near Charlotte. While it once promoted militia-style themes, it now claims to engage only in Bible study.

Ohio. The first few months of 1995 were marked by the widespread organizing throughout the state of the "Ohio Unorganized Militia"—loose-knit groups that conduct various paramilitary exercises. However, low attendance at meetings since the Oklahoma City bombing suggests that the militia movement in Ohio may have lost some strength. The Ohio Unorganized Militia has justified its activity by citing the U.S. Constitution's Second Amendment and a provision of the Ohio Revised Code that provides for an "unorganized militia...of all able-bodied citizens of the state who are more than 17 years of age and not more than 67 years of age." The group has been active in Franklin, Brown, Clermont, Hamilton, Stark, Coshocton, Columbiana, Williams, Lucas, Medina, and Montgomery counties.

Despite the claimed legal basis for its existence, the militia has used highly inflammatory language. Rod Scott, a captain in the Brown County group, has stated: "Any armed agent of the United States government who comes to my home or any militia member's home to take a gun, to steal my property, to violate my freedom, will be met with deadly force."

Oklahoma. The most visible group, the Oklahoma Citizens Militia, operates in Eufaula, southeast of Tulsa, under the leadership of denture maker Ross Hullett. He condemned the Oklahoma City bombing, stating, "Christians don't do this to people." Nevertheless, Oklahoma militia members share the characteristic, paradoxical "patriotism" of the broader movement. "I would lay down my life for my country," member John Harrell told *The Wall Street Journal*, "but I wouldn't spit on a congressman if he were burning to death."

Oregon. Touting the familiar theme that "a Civilian Militia is a

"The first few months of 1995 were marked by the widespread organizing throughout the state of the "Ohio Unorganized Militia..."

final line of defense against all enemies both foreign and domestic," the Central Oregon Regional Militia has operated modest units in the town of Prineville and neighboring Deschutes County. The Salem-based Northwest Oregon Regional Militia was disbanded by its founder, insurance salesman Mike Cross, following the Oklahoma City bombing. Cross said he feared persecution by the Federal government. He stated, "If they would blow up one of their own buildings, who knows what they could do to militias."

Pennsylvania. Sporadic militia organizing has been conducted throughout eastern and southeastern Pennsylvania, including Dauphin, Delaware, Bucks, Berks, Montgomery, and Chester counties. Some of this activity may have been spurred in part by the Nov. 20, 1994, recruiting speech in suburban Philadelphia by Samuel Sherwood, head of the Idaho-based United States Militia Association, who subsequently appeared on local talk radio programs.

In Crawford County in the western part of the state, a Feb. 4, 1995, appearance by Michigan militia proponent Mark Koernke attracted various militia sympathizers and groups. The Keystone Militia has a base in adjacent Warren County. Militias also have formed in Potter and Elk counties in north central Pennsylvania. The Potter County-based Bucktail Militia (named after Civil War sharpshooters who trained in the area) claims "brigades" in neighboring counties.

South Carolina. In the early months of 1995, the South Carolina Civilian Militia began actively recruiting in the Greenville-Spartanburg area, seeking, in particular, pilots and those with military skills. The militia's self-proclaimed leader, Ian Roebuck, a preacher, claims 80 members in several counties. Roebuck and information officer R.C. Davenport disavow any ties with white supremacist organizations, but advance the notion that the U.S. is on course to succumb to a United Nations-led tyranny.

South Dakota. The Rapid City-based Tri-State Militia is described by its leader Rodger Chant as an umbrella organization for militia groups across the state. He also says that the group maintains ties with 35 other militias across the country, including the Michigan Militia.

Tennessee. George Etter of Morristown leads the pro-militia Christian Civil Liberties Association. He publishes a newsletter, *The Militia News*, which he claims circulates to millions of militia members and reportedly distributes materials that explain how to make automatic weapons and explosives. Additionally, a militia has been reported to be operating near Memphis.

Texas. An active militia presence was established in Texas with the founding of the Texas Constitutional Militia in 1994. The organization'smanual includes language identical to the Michigan Militia's literature,with a pledge to "stand against tyranny, globalism, moral relativism, humanism, and the New World Order threatening to undermine our form of government and these United States of America." The Texas Constitutional Militia has organized widely, with groups active in the San Antonio, Dallas, Houston, and Beaumont areas. A separate group, the Red River Militia (or Red River Militia Guard), has organized in east Texas, and is believed to be active in Gilmore, Marshall, DeKalb, and Texarkana. The Dallas-area militia, known as the North Texas Constitutional Militia and based in suburban Richardson, has engaged in paramilitary and survival exercises near the Texas-Oklahoma border. These exercises have included the STAR (Strategic Training for Assistance and Readiness) program. According to its material, STAR is conducted by a "cadre" of "former Rangers, Seals, Green Berets, and Martial Arts Experts." On April 19, 1995, the day of the Oklahoma City bombing, and two years to the day after the Branch Davidian compound at Waco erupted in flames, the North Texas Constitutional Militia erected a stone tablet near the site of the compound in memory of those killed in the blaze.

Several militias also are believed to be active in Kerrville, northwest of San Antonio, among them the U.S. Civil Militia, founded by Betty Schier and her son Carl. In early May, they turned over to Federal authorities a variety of explosives, including TNT, nitroglycerine, and a homemade material incorporating ammonium nitrate and paraffin. Betty Schier, a retired gun dealer, said she and her son "don't condone" the Oklahoma City bombing, and claimed they only had the explosives for purposes of producing a video called "The Mad Bomber" that he has been trying to sell through a survivalist magazine. The authorities questioned the pair and took possession of the explosives after Carl Schier alerted the FBI that an acquaintance had asked him for information on making a car bomb. No charges were filed against the Schiers.

On Feb. 18, 1995, Bo Gritz brought his SPIKE weapons and survival training workshop to Dallas. Several anti-Semitic publications were sold at the seminar, including *The Protocols of the Elders' of Zion*; *Jewish Ritual Murder*, by mid-century British anti-Semite Arnold Leese; *The Jews and Their Lies*, by Martin Luther; and *The Truth About the Protocols*, by Gerald Winrod, the Kansas-based Jew-hating demagogue of the 1930s and 1940s known as the "Jayhawk Nazi."

In an official letter dated March 22, 1995, Rep. Stockman wrote to Attorney General Janet Reno claiming that "reliable sources" had informed him that several Federal agencies were preparing a paramilitary style attack on the militias, whom he described as "Americans who pose no risk to others." Stockman even specified the dates and hour of the alleged impending attack: March 25 or 26 at 4:00 a.m.

Warning that the assault would "run the risk of an irreparable breach between the Federal government and the public," Stockman asked for detailed information about the military arrangements for the assault. The purported plan of attack, it turned out, was a fiction.

Stockman also wrote an article that appeared in the June, 1995, issue of *Guns and Ammo* magazine, maintaining that the raid on the Branch Davidian compound in Waco was conducted by the Clinton Administration "to prove the need for a ban on so-called assault weapons." Earlier, Stockman appeared as a guest on the radio program of Liberty Lobby, the leading anti-Semitic propaganda group in the nation; he since has maintained he was unaware of Liberty Lobby's anti-Semitism.

Utah. News accounts citing law enforcement sources report that at least seven militia units are operating in Utah. One, the Box Elder County-based Unorganized State Militia of Utah, was disbanded in the spring of 1995 by leader Doug Christiansen, who said he disapproved of the growing militancy of the movement.

Johnny Bangerter, the leader of a St. George-based neo-Nazi Skinhead group called the Army of Israel, claims his organization has ties to militias in Montana, Texas, and Utah. He and other Skinheads traveled to northern Idaho in 1992 to express support for white supremacist Randy Weaver during his standoff with Federal law enforcement agents—an event that later contributed to the genesis of the militia movement.

"...the Box Elder County-based Unorganized State Militia of Utah, was disbanded in the spring of 1995..."

Virginia. James Roy Mullins, a founding member of the militia-like Blue Ridge Hunt Club, pled guilty to Federal firearm offenses on Feb. 27, 1995. On May 15, he was sentenced to a five-year prison term. In Bedford County, pastor and gun dealer William Waters claims to lead the 1st Virginia Freeborn Civilian Militia. Douglas Jeffreys, a state highway department worker from Hanover County, says that he has been touring the state working to form the Virginia Citizens' Militia, an organization of loosely affiliated groups.

Washington has been the site of frequent recruitment and organizing drives by militia groups based outside the state. Militias have emerged throughout the state, particularly in the counties surrounding Seattle, in the Spokane area, and in Clark and Cowlitz counties in southwestern Washington.

West Virginia. The leading militia figure in the state is Ray Looker, whose group, the Mountaineer Militia, holds periodic meetings. Echoing the oft-repeated militia story that mysterious unmarked black helicopters are spying on leaders of the movement around the country, Looker claimed that they have circled over his home in the Clarksburg area. He also has asserted that the West Virginia National Guard has been denied ammunition by the Federal government.

Wisconsin. The Militia of Wisconsin (also known as Freeman Militia of Wisconsin) is an amalgam of three small organizations—one under the leadership of Don Treloar in Waupaca County, one in Vernon County under Will Holzli, and a third near Slinger. Unified around the pro-gun, anti-government, conspiracy-driven philosophies that characterize other militia groups, they meet regularly and claim to engage in weapons training and maneuvers. Treloar, speaking of the group's regular field exercises, says "we are preparing men for battle." Holzli, who called media within hours of the Oklahoma City bombing to say that he thought it might be part of a government plot, has boasted of 10,000 members statewide, a plainly exaggerated claim.

Wyoming. The Western United Militia (WUM), a small group based in Cheyenne, is led by Robert Becker, identified as "Col. Becker" in WUM materials. The group has advertised for recruits in a free shopper's weekly in Cheyenne, and a WUM flier was distributed at a Cheyenne gun show in May, 1995. Headed "Patriots Unite!," the handbill contends that Pres. Clinton, the UN, and other global conspirators seek to establish a one-world government, and that—presumably toward this end—Soviet-built tanks are being transported to various U.S. locations. The flier makes the (certainly exaggerated) claim that WUM has "21 divisions in 17 Western States" and instructs would-be members to enclose $20 with their applications.

In Sweetwater County, in southwestern Wyoming, leaflets headed "Wyoming Militia" have surfaced, possibly indicating some local activity. The materials cite several laws as justifying the militia's existence.

They also offer, for use in unsecured telephone communications, suggested code words for "enemy," "contraband," "weapons," and "making or using explosives." Recommended reading includes such titles as *The Ultimate Sniper* and *Can You Survive?*—the latter work written by Robert B. DePugh, who served time in prison for firearms violations and other offenses related to activity with the Minutemen, a heavily armed, far-right group he founded in the 1960s. Other names that appear on the leaflets include "Sweetwater Citizen Emergency Response Group" and "Wyoming 'Unorganized' (Reserve) Militia, 4th Group."

Volatile Mix in Viper Militia: Hatred Plus a Love for Guns[4]

PHOENIX, July 3—On West Shangri-La Road, a quiet street where children pedal bicycles past ornamental cactuses and yellow desert blooms, the two men living at number 6748 led a suburban life that was, well, different.

Dean C. Pleasant used to paint camouflage patterns on hand grenades and leave them in his backyard to dry.

His housemate, Randy L. Nelson, a house painter who called himself the Captain of the Viper Militia, slept with his beloved "Shirley," a Browning machine gun mounted on the headboard of his bed.

Searching the trim white-and-blue bungalow in the suburb of Peoria on Monday, Federal agents, according to court papers, found a small armory tucked into dressers and stacked in closets: grenades, fuses, blasting caps, 2 pistols, 2 machine guns, 6 rifles and 56 boxes crammed with 11,463 rounds of ammunition. On the living room coffee table was a how-to manual called "Domestic Disturbances."

Today, the 2 roommates, along with 10 other members of the Vipers paramilitary group, are in jail here, facing charges that include illegal possession of a machine gun and conspiracy to teach bombing techniques to provoke civil disorder.

A largely blue-collar mix of high school graduates and dropouts, all the Vipers are white, have no significant criminal records and are stuck in low-paying jobs.

They include two janitors, a used-furniture salesman, an AT&T billing representative, an air conditioner repairman, a doughnut baker, an engineer and the doorman for Tiffany Cabaret, a Phoenix topless bar. Experts say they roughly reflect the demographics of the anti-government paramilitary movement. Their defenders say the Vipers are merely Walter Mitty types—weekend warriors who conducted harmless war games in the desert. In this vein, they say, the Government will have a hard time winning any conspiracy convictions.

"Where the heck is the conspiracy?" asked Scott Grainger, a longtime friend of Mr. Pleasant. "I thought you had to have a plan. It's not illegal to go out and blow up rocks in the desert."

Noting that the arrests came barely a week after the deadly bombing at an American military base in Saudi Arabia, Mr. Grainger, who is the county chairman here of the Libertarian Party, said he suspected political motives behind the highly publicized crackdown on a group that Federal agents had been monitoring for seven months.

---

[4]Article by James Brooke, from *The New York Times* A1 Jl 5, '96. Copyright © 1996 The New York Times Company. Reprinted with permission.

Questioning the timing, Mr.Grainger asked, "These guys have been around for a while. Why pick on them now?"

In contrast, prosecutors paint the Vipers as an urban terror cell that was ready, and able, to cause havoc as great as that caused in the Oklahoma City bombing last year. To bolster this view, they plan to show a videotape in court here on Friday during bail hearings for the group's members.

The videotape was shot two years ago by Mr. Pleasant, the indictment says, and takes viewers on a walking tour of seven local, state and Federal buildings and a television station in the Phoenix area. With Mr. Pleasant providing some of the narration, the tape instructs viewers on how to place charges by support columns to "collapse" the government buildings.

In addition to editing an urban guerrilla tape, Mr. Pleasant, 27, has left the longest paper trail of the dozen detainees. Through letters to the editor, political campaign statements and a gun lovers newsletter that he edited, an ideological portrait emerges of Mr. Pleasant, who, until last week, regularly served as the host for Viper meetings in the living room of his rented house here.

"...the three friends formed the nucleus of a paramilitary group they called the Viper Militia."

Viscerally opposed to government controls, Mr. Pleasant once told The *Phoenix Gazette*, a local newspaper, that he had carried a concealed pistol without a permit since he was 16.

In 1992, when Paul Johnson, then Mayor of Phoenix, proposed an ordinance banning minors from owning or carrying firearms, Mr. Pleasant wrote to the Gazette, saying: "Mayor Johnson is looking down the big bore of Arizona law, with gun enthusiasts, their finger on the trigger, saying, 'Go ahead. Make my day!'"

Treasuring his "Tommy" gun, a Thompson machine gun capable of firing 500 rounds a minute, Mr. Pleasant waged a constant battle against advocates of gun control.

"If one's aim is to lessen violent crime, what makes the editor think that a murderer will be any less vicious with a machete?" he said inanother letter to the Gazette, in 1992. "To blame objects for the evil that people do to each other is socially irresponsible."

In 1994, Mr. Pleasant was living at his parents' house here and studying at a local community college when agents from the Bureau of Alcohol, Tobacco and Firearms knocked on the door, wanting to ask questions about his recent gun trades.

Furious, Mr. Pleasant refused to cooperate, recalled a friend, Ernest Hancock. A few days later, around May 30, 1994, he and a married couple, Ellen and David W. Belliveau, started filming Government buildings in Phoenix, including the firearms bureau's office. Later, the three friends formed the nucleus of a paramilitary group they called the Viper Militia.

The Viper name, a rallying symbol for the paramilitary movement, is believed to be a salute to the Revolutionary War-era rattlesnake flag, which carried the warning, "Don't Tread on Me!"

In a parallel protest strategy, Mr. Pleasant, already an officer in the local Libertarian Party chapter, decided to fight big government by running for a seat in the Arizona State Senate.

Describing taxes as "legalized theft," the Libertarian candidate
called for an end to firearms controls and mandatory auto insurance.

"The No. 1 thing I want to see done is the repeal of state-man-
dated auto insurance," he told *The Arizona Republic* newspaper. In
1991, he spent 31 days in jail for driving without insurance and
without license plates.

To his opponent, John Kaites, Mr. Pleasant, a college student who-
moonlighted as a doughnut baker, seemed "a bit immature—a
25-year-old kid that got satisfaction out of carrying a concealed
weapon," Mr. Kaites said. "He never seemed to have grown out of
the G.I. Joe phase," he added.

"He told me that the government should not be in the business of
regulating schools, building roads, outlawing narcotic substances or
controlling weapons," Mr. Kaites recalled today.

*"...A.T.F. agents
found a booby-trap
device, camouflage
clothing, a pistol,
three rifles,
4,000 rounds of
ammunition and
his machine gun."*

When Kaites campaign signs started to disappear, only to reap-
pear as Pleasant campaign signs, Mr. Kaites called the candidate's
mother, Gloria, to complain. The expensive plywood signs stopped
vanishing.

Mr. Kaites, a Republican, won the two-man race—with 24,780
votes to 7,013 for the Libertarian.

When reached by telephone today, Mrs. Pleasant declined to talk
about her son, saying only, "We love Dean and know he's a good
guy and would not hurt anybody."

After losing the election, Mr. Pleasant left home, dropped out of
college and got a low-paying job as a sales clerk in an Army surplus
store. Two months ago, he was dismissed for poor performance,
which included petty theft, said Scott Peterson, the store's owner.

Until Mr. Pleasant's arrest, his real passion was his after-hours
life, which largely revolved around guns, explosives and parumili-
tary training. In his bedroom on Monday, A.T.F. agents found a
booby-trap device, camouflage clothing, a pistol, three rifles, 4,000
rounds of ammunition and his machine gun.

"He had a very dim view of what the government was doing to
people's rights," recalled Alan Trabilcy, owner of Outpost Firearms
and Ammunition, a store where Mr. Pleasant was a frequent cus-
tomer this year.

Not particularly discreet about his paramilitary activities, Mr.
Pleasant sometimes wore Viper insignia patches outside his home.
Last March, he was listed on an Internet page called Restoring
America as a paramilitary contact for newcomers moving to the
Phoenix area.

When guns were involved, his comrade in arms was his
32-year-old housemate, Mr. Nelson. The rowdier of the pair, Mr.
Nelson often appeared at gun events wearing camouflage pants and
obscene T-shirts.

"He was just a youngster who dressed outrageously and acted
that way sometimes," said Terry Allison, president of the Arizona
Rifle and Pistol Association, a club that counted Mr. Nelson and his
housemate among its 2,000 members. "But he wasn't subversive in

any way."

Last September, Mr. Nelson and Mr. Pleasant were kicked out of a shooting competition sponsored in Las Vegas, Nev., by Soldier of Fortune magazine.

"We were too rowdy for *Soldier of Fortune*," Mr. Pleasant wrote later in a gun enthusiast's bulletin that he edited, *SHF Shooting Sports Newsletter*. "Aren't those the guys who frag Serbs for giggles? The same guys who went to Rhodesia to shoot black folk because their Vietnam playground wasn't available any more?"

Mr. Nelson, who styles himself as Captain of the Vipers, seethed over his rejection by the competition's organizer, Michael Horne.

"Next year, I'm not gonna shoot, just so I can get a chance to catch you alone and smash your face," he wrote about Mr. Horne in the semimonthly bulletin.

This paramilitary leader, a bachelor who slept with his gun Shirley, wrote of trying "to satisfy that primal urge that makes you want to kill."

"You low crawl into the bedroom of one of your roommates and sneak right up to his bed," he wrote. "You press your .45 to his temple and...damn! Not again, waited too long and now the urge is gone!"

Antiabortion Extremists:
Organized and Dangerous[5]

Like the rest of the nation, I watched in horror as the Oklahoma City tragedy and its investigation unfolded last spring. But unlike many Americans, I did not have a "this can't have happened here" reaction. As a defender of abortion clinics, I know that it can—and has. Women's health clinics have been savaged by domestic terrorism. Since 1977, there have been at least 40 clinic bombings, 100 instances of arson, 400 death threats and stalkings, 11 attempted murders and five murders, according to surveys by the National Abortion Federation and my organization, the Feminist Majority Foundation.

More important, many of these acts cannot be dismissed as the work of "lone crazies." Those who threaten and kill doctors do not act in a vacuum: they are surrounded by a network of extremists, many of whom say the murders are justifiable.

Connective links between separate episodes of clinic violence abound. Take the murder of Dr. John Bayard Britton in Pensacola, Florida, last summer. Paul Hill, the man convicted of the crime, was the only person to fire shots that day. But according to the militant antiabortion magazine *Life Advocate*, Dr. Briton had earlier been staked out and photographed by *four* activists, including Hill. Among the other stalkers was John Burt, a director of the group Rescue America, who is being sued for conspiracy in the murder of Dr. Britton's predecessor, Dr. David Gunn.

Antiabortion vandalism too, often occurs in patterns: in the early 1990s, scores of clinics around the country experienced near-identical butyric-acid attacks within hours or days of one another. Chance? Maybe not. One manual, titled *The Army of God*, contains directions for such assaults and was found in the backyard of activist Shelley Shannon, who has been convicted of the attempted murder of a Wichita, Kansas physician as well as ten other clinic-related felonies. The manual, Shannon has said, is circulated among extremists.

The Justice Department formed a task force last year to look into the possibility of an organized movement promoting clinic violence. But in general, the public, political leaders and law enforcement have tended to treat such acts as unconnected—looking solely at the perpetrators rather than at the group ties. Police, for instance, did not research Shelley Shannon's home for evidence of possible conspiracy until almost six weeks after her arrest for attempted murder. Why the lethargy? Perhaps we write off antiabortion extremists as single-issue zealots—otherwise peaceful individuals

---

[5]Article by Eleanor Smeal, president of the Feminist Majority Foundation from *Glamour* 93:148 O '95. Copyright © 1995 Eleanor Smeal. Reprinted with permission.

driven mad only by the passion of their pro-life feelings. If *I* am not a doctor, this thinking goes, then these nuts are no threat to me.

That couldn't be more wrong. Some antiabortion extremists overlap in ideology and strategy with members of the private militia movement; Rep. Charles Schumer (D-N.Y.) recently held congressional hearings on possible links between the two. Both groups harp on common themes: the need to take up arms to defend so-called persecuted Christians, identification with the Branch Davidians who died at Waco, antifeminism, antiSemitism (one antiabortion pamphlet includes jokes about killing doctors, who are caricatured as Jews), antigay dogma and an attempt at a theological justification for a fundamentalist Christian takeover of the United States.

Some militia members view the government's legalization of abortion as one of its prime offenses. Consider the 100-page *Field Manual Section I: Principles Justifying the Arming and Organizing of a Militia*. Published by the underground Free Militia, the manual lists several civil rights supposedly being eroded by the federal government. What is the first right listed? Not the right to bear arms, as one might think, but the *right to life*—threatened, the manual says, by legal abortion.

"...I believe these groups watch one another; cracking down on one sends a message to all."

In turn, some violent antiabortion groups employ antigovernment invective. *Life Advocate* alleges that the Justice Department is attempting a "political purge of those on the Right" and charges that "believers in the Second Amendment...and pro-lifers" are targets of a future Waco-like "final solution."

And the two movements, while far from identical, do share adherents. Last year Matthew Trewhella, a cofounder of the group Missionaries to the Preborn, spoke to the ultraconservative U.S. Taxpayers Party about paramilitary groups. "This Christmas," Trewhella says on a videotape obtained by the Planned Parenthood Federation of America, "I want you to do the most loving thing. I want you to buy each of your children an SKS rifle and 500 rounds of ammunition."

Since the Oklahoma City tragedy, I have asked myself many questions: Could we have stopped the escalation of clinic terrorism if we had reacted to the first bombings with greater outrage? What if we had turned the same critical eye to militant antiabortion groups that we are now applying to private militias? Could we possibly have *prevented* Oklahoma City by sending a strong and uncompromising message to all kinds of terrorists that their lawless acts would not be tolerated? That may sound far-fetched, but I believe these groups watch one another; cracking down on one sends a message to all.

Now that we have a glimpse of where terrorism leads, we must probe it in all its forms. Political debates in a democracy, whether over abortion or the size and reach of government, must be settled by the ballot box, not the cartridge box.

III. The Effects of Terrorism

Editor's Introduction

A terrorist action is an event that affects many levels of society. In the aftermath of bloodshed, there may be a flurry of responses from politicians, a claiming of "credit" by one or another underground group, fears of copycat actions, and well-publicized police investigations. All of these consequences extend the meaning of a given terrorist act and demonstrate its far-reaching effects.

Writing only a few days after the Oklahoma City Federal Building bombing, in April of 1995, Rowan Scarborough, in "Terrorism Gives U.S. Wakeup Call," provides a sampling of the immediate reactions by politicians and others in key federal positions. Most of those quoted in the article express a "deep concern about terrorism *in* the United States" and call for an immediate change in government policy to reflect the rapid rise of terrorist activity within American borders.

Following a terrorist action, it is not uncommon for someone to claim responsibility. In April of 1995, *The New York Times* received a letter from a so-called "Group FC," who seemed extremely well-informed about a series of deadly mail bombings. The letter is now attributed to Theodore J. Kaczynski, the alleged Unabomber. More articulate than most terrorist communications, it is nevertheless typical in its overriding concern "to win acceptance for certain ideas" and in its chilling arrogance.

The third article, "First the Flame Then the Blame," by Jack E. White from *Time,* looks at the investigations that followed a series of suspicious fires at African-American churches in the South. The author explains how the ministers of these churches believe that federal investigators are traveling down the wrong avenues in their search for culprits and are blaming the victims, despite a long history of racist violence against African-American congregations.

While investigations may rage, politicians talk, and various groups lay claim for a terrorist event, the most important after-effect is the continued suffering of the innocent. The last article in this section, "One Year Later: The Family That Triumphed over Terrorism," highlights the physical horror of the Oklahoma City bombing and portrays a family determined to survive its devastating effects. Personal tragedy is often sometimes lost amid the headlines, the politics, and the accusations. This piece has been included as a stark image of the very real suffering caused by terrorist activities such as the bombing of the Oklahoma Federal Building.

Terrorism Gives U.S. Wakeup Call[1]

Experts call for stricter policies

America's heartland discovered a brutal reality yesterday: No one in the United States is safe from terrorism.

Two years ago, a bomb underneath the World Trade Center erupted amid the crowded, anonymous chaos of New York City.

"We're going to have to start thinking defensive about these things, and that is not a happy prospect," said Rep. Henry J. Hyde, Illinois Republican and chairman of the House Judiciary Committee, which plans to write an anti-terrorism statute.

"We're vulnerable," Mr. Hyde said. "America is a free country. It's like a hotel lobby. It's easy to get in and easy to get out. I have seen the Capitol change from an open place where tourists could wander around aimlessly to a place where you get frisked when you go in."

Terrorism experts yesterday offered lists of defensive tactics that governments and businesses might employ to make the country less vulnerable. The options include tighter building security, tougher immigration policies and better intelligence to nip terrorist operations in the bud.

"We have to harden our sites of opportunity," said Neil Livingston, who has written extensively on international terrorism. "We have to take a look at the security systems at buildings and maybe close off underground parking that allows you to get too close to these buildings. We have to look at no longer permitting jeeps, vans and trucks in underground garages because they can carry too much explosives. The second thing you have to do is increase intelligence, both domestic and international."

Mayer Nudell, executive director of the International Association of Counter-Terrorists and Security Professionals, said the U.S. Immigration and Naturalization Service needs to start monitoring foreigners who enter this country on visa.

"They have the power to do it. The problem is they are not," Mr. Nudell said. "That is an area I think we ought to look at, especially if we have intelligence that these people might be involved with terrorists."

Sheik Oman Abdel-Rahman, the Muslim cleric now on trial on charges of masterminding the World Trade Center car-bombing, allegedly entered the United States under false pretenses in 1990. At the time the bomb went off, the sheik was the subject of drawn-out proceedings aimed at deporting him.

Mr. Nudell said it is not always easy to monitor visa-holders. He said universities often object to giving the government information about a foreign student.

---

[1]Article by Rowan Scarborough, from *The Washington Times* A1 Ap 24, '95. Copyright © 1995 News World Communications, Inc. Reprinted with permission.

He said the FBI used to check on suspected Russian spies by finding out what they were reading at public libraries. But eventually the libraries objected, citing civil liberties. "That's one example of one hand getting in the way of the other," he said. "One civil liberty gets in the way of protecting all our civil liberties."

Mr. Nudell said the FBI should infiltrate terrorist organizations the way police penetrate drug gangs.

In testimony less than two weeks ago before Mr. Hyde's committee, FBI Director Louis Freeh predicted more acts of terrorism such as the one in Oklahoma City.

"I am deeply concerned about terrorism in the United States," he said in prepared remarks. "The face and the hand of terrorism are changing dramatically as we enter the last half of the last decade before the 21st century."

"In recent years, we have not witnessed significant state-sponsored terrorist activity in this country," he added. "But this could change if countries which sponsor terrorism decide to include terrorism within U.S. borders on their agendas."

Mr. Freeh, whose agency has lead responsibility for stopping domestic terrorism, asked Congress to give him "new tools and resources to fight its serpent-like presence around the world" and make the U.S. "a hostile environment for terrorists."

In a call for tougher immigration laws, the federal government's top cop told the story of a foreigner who entered the country on a visa. Calling the visitor "Y," Mr. Freeh said the person maintained a major role in a known terrorist organization throughout his stay in the United States.

But he said the FBI was powerless to have "Y" deported because he did not violate any of his visa's requirements. To present evidence against him at a public deportation hearing would have caused "irreparable harm to the national security," he said.

Bombing in Sacramento:
The Letter[2]

Following are excerpts of the letter received by *The New York Times* on Monday from the self-designated terrorist group FC, claiming responsibility for the serial bombings that the Federal Bureau of Investigation attributes to a single person or group in the case known as Unabom. The document is presented verbatim, with original spelling, emphasis and punctuation. Three passages have been deleted at the request of the F.B.I.

[Passage deleted at the request of the F.B.I.]

This is a message from the terrorist group FC.

We blew up Thomas Mosser last December because he was a Burston-Marsteller executive. Among other misdeeds, Burston-Marsteller helped Exxon clean up its public image after the Exxon Valdez incident. But we attacked Burston-Marsteller less for its specific misdeeds than on general principles. Burston-Marsteller is about the biggest organization in the public relations field. This means that its business is the development of techniques for manipulating people's attitudes. It was for this more than for its actions in specific cases that we sent a bomb to an executive of this company.

Some news reports have made the misleading statement that we have been attacking universities or scholars. We have nothing against universities or scholars as such. All the university people whom we have attacked have been specialists in technical fields. (We consider certain areas of applied psychology, such as behavior modification, to be technical fields.) We would not want anyone to think that we have any desire to hurt professors who study archaeology, history, literature or harmless stuff like that. The people we are out to get are the scientists and engineers, especially in critical fields like computers and genetics. As for the bomb planted in the Business School at the U. of Utah, that was a botched operation. We won't say how or why it was botched because we don't want to give the FBI any clues. No one was hurt by that bomb.

In our previous letter to you we called ourselves anarchists. Since 'anarchist' is a vague word that has been applied to a variety of attitudes, further explanation is needed. We call ourselves anarchists because we would like, ideally, to break down all society into very small, completely autonomous units. Regrettably, we don't see any clear road to this goal, so we leave it to the indefinite future. Our more immediate goal, which we think may be attainable at some time during the next several decades, is the destruction of the worldwide industrial system. Through our bombings we hope to

---

[2]Article from *The New York Times* A16 Ap 26, '95. Copyright © 1995 The New York Times Company. Reprinted with permission.

promote social instability in industrial society, propagate anti-industrial ideas and give encouragement to those who hate the industrial system.

The FBI has tried to portray these bombings as the work of an isolated nut. We won't waste our time arguing about whether we are nuts, but we certainly are not isolated. For security reasons we won't reveal the number of members of our group, but anyone who will read the anarchist and radical environmentalist journals will see that opposition to the industrial-technological system is widespread and growing.

Why do we announce our goals only now, through we made our first bomb some seventeen years ago? Our early bombs were too ineffectual to attract much public attention or give encouragement to those who hate the system. We found by experience that gunpowder bombs, if small enough to be carried inconspicuously, were too feeble to do much damage, so we took a couple of years off to do some experimenting. We learned how to make pipe bombs that were powerful enough, and we used these in a couple of successful bombings as well as in some unsuccessful ones.

[Passage deleted at the request of the F.B.I.]

"We have a long article, between 29,000 and 37,000 words, that we want to have published."

Since we no longer have to confine the explosive in a pipe, we are now free of limitations on the size and shape of our bombs. We are pretty sure we know how to increase the power of our explosives and reduce the number of batteries needed to set them off. And, as we've just indicated, we think we now have more effective fragmentation material. So we expect to be able to pack deadly bombs into ever smaller, lighter and more harmless looking packages. On the other hand, we believe we will be able to make bombs much bigger than any we've made before. With a briefcase-full or a suitcase-full of explosives we should be able to blow out the walls of substantial buildings.

Clearly we are in a position to do a great deal of damage. And it doesn't appear that the FBI is going to catch us any time soon. The FBI is a joke.

The people who are pushing all this growth and progress garbage deserve to be severely punished. But our goal is less to punish them than to propagate ideas. Anyhow we are getting tired of making bombs. It's no fun having to spend all your evenings and weekends preparing dangerous mixtures, filing trigger mechanisms out of scraps of metal or searching the sierras for a place isolated enough to test a bomb. So we offer a bargain.

We have a long article, between 29,000 and 37,000 words, that we want to have published. If you can get it published according to our requirements we will permanently desist from terrorist activities. It must be published in the New York Times, Time or Newsweek, or in some other widely read, nationally distributed periodical. Because of its length we suppose it will have to be serialized. Alternatively, it can be published as a small book, but the book must be well publicized and made available at a moderate price in bookstores nationwide and in at least some places abroad. Whoever agrees to publish the material will have exclusive rights to reproduce it for a period of six months and will be welcome to any profits they may make from it. After six months from the first appearance of the article or book it must become public property, so that anyone can reproduce or publish it. (If material is serialized, first instalment becomes public property six months after appearance of first instalment, second instalment, etc.) We must have the right to publish in the New York Times, Time or Newsweek, each year for three years after the appearance of our article or book, three thousand words expanding or clarifying our material or rebutting criticisms of it.

The article will not explicitly advocate violence. There will be an unavoidable implication that we favor violence to the extent that it may be necessary, since we advocate eliminating industrial society and we ourselves have been using violence to that end. But the article will not advocate violence explicitly, nor will it propose the overthrow of the United States Government, nor will it contain obscenity or anything else that you would be likely to regard as unacceptable for publication.

How do you know that we will keep our promise to desist from terrorism if our conditions are met? It will be to our advantage to keep our promise. We want to win acceptance for certain ideas. If we break our promise people will lose respect for us and so will be less likely to accept the ideas.

Our offer to desist from terrorism is subject to three qualifications. First: Our promise to desist will not take effect until all parts of our article or book have appeared in print. Second: If the authorities should succeed in tracking us down and an attempt is made to arrest any of us, or even to question us in connection with the bombings, we reserve the right to use violence. Third: We distinguish between terrorism and sabotage. By terrorism we mean actions motivated by a desire to influence the development of a society and intended to cause injury or death to human beings. By sabotage we mean similarly motivated actions intended to destroy property without injuring human beings. The promise we offer is to desist from terrorism. We reserve the right to engage in sabotage.

It may be just as well that failure of our early bombs discouraged us from making any public statements at that time. We were very young then and our thinking was crude. Over the years we have given as much attention to the development of our ideas as to the development of bombs, and we now have something serious to say. And we feel that just now the time is ripe for the presentation of anti-industrial ideas.

Please see to it that the answer to our offer is well publicized in the media so that we won't miss it. Be sure to tell us where and how our material will be published and how long it will take to appear in print once we have sent in the manuscript. If the answer is satisfactory, we will finish typing the manuscript and send it to you. If the answer is unsatisfactory, we will start building our next bomb.

"...Our promise to desist will not take effect until all parts of our article or book have appeared in print."

We encourage you to print this letter. FC
[Passage deleted at the request of the F.B.I.]

First the Flame, Then the Blame[3]

When he first saw the smoldering ruins of his Macedonia Missionary Baptist Church in Fruitvale, Tennessee, on Jan. 13, 1995, the Rev. Sherron Eugene Brown could not imagine anything worse. Then, the agents from the Bureau of Alcohol, Tobacco and Firearms went to work on him. "They took me and the church treasurer to the federal building, put us in two separate rooms and asked us all kinds of questions about our insurance policies, about whether we were behind in paying off our mortgage or if any members of the congregation were angry," Brown remembers. "They were acting as if we had set our own church on fire."

As of last week—when the Rising Sun Missionary Baptist church in Greensboro, Alabama, and a former sanctuary at Matthews-Murkland Presbyterian Church in Charlotte, North Carolina, were torched—30 black churches in an eight-state arc from Louisiana to Virginia had been burned over the past 18 months. Only a handful of these arson cases have been solved. Such senseless destruction strikes at the soul of congregations. But their anguish deepens when they, the victims, also become suspects.

As Attorney General Janet Reno and Treasury Secretary Robert Rubin will hear in meetings this week with the pastors of several burned-out churches, such misguided scrutiny has been occurring all too frequently in the federal investigation of the fires. Dozens of pastors charge that despite the long history of racist terrorism throughout the region, investigators are not vigorously pursuing the possibility that the fires were set by white hate groups. Instead, the ministers charge, they, their families and their congregations have been subjected to harsh interrogation, lie-detector tests and harassment at their homes and jobs. In one instance, a 17-year-old female member of the Rev. Algie Jarret's Mount Calvary Baptist Church in Bolivar, Tennessee, was taken out of a classroom by an FBI agent and questioned so roughly that she broke down in tears. Says Jarrett: "He tried to make her say something that wasn't true."

"In most cases the lines of inquiry with regard to white supremacists are not being followed by any of the authorities," charges the Rev. Mac Charles Jones, associate general secretary for racial justice of the National Council of Churches, who has visited dozens of burned-out churches over the past three months. "The questioning has been about problems in the churches, about the pastors, about the churches' money or insurance. That was the first line of inquiry, and sometimes it has been the only one."

This is an unsettling allegation. If Jones and the other ministers are right, hundreds of agents from the AFT, FBI and state agencies

---

[3]Article by Jack E. White, from *Time* 147:35 Je 17, '96. Copyright © 1996 TIME, INC. Reprinted with permission.

have been chasing after scapegoats rather than real culprits. The issue surfaced at a hearing last month by the House Judiciary Committee in testimony from witnesses as diverse as Joseph Lowery of the Southern Christian Leadership Conference and the Rev. Earl W. Jackson Jr. of the Christian Coalition. But their charges came only after several high-ranking officials from the Department of Justice, the FBI and the ATF denied that they had received any complaints about the focus of the investigations.

There is clearly more here than a color-coded difference of opinion. Either the ministers are grossly exaggerating their mistreatment or top Clinton Administration officials are not getting adequate information about their agents' conduct in the field. Deval Patrick, the Assistant Attorney General for Civil Rights, insists that every lead is being followed. And he notes that in several cases whites with ties to racist groups have been convicted and sent to prison. Indeed, last week a Baptist congregation in South Carolina opened a new front against the terrorists by filing a civil damage suit accusing the Christian Knights of the Ku Klux Klan of being responsible for torching their church.

"...South Carolina opened a new front against the terrorists by filing a civil damage suit..."

The real problem is deep-seated black suspicion of law enforcement that dates back to the days when J. Edgar Hoover's FBI put more zeal into collecting dirt on Martin Luther King Jr. than into protecting civil-rights workers. It does not help that two ATF agents who face potential disciplinary action for taking part in the racist shenanigans at the so-called Good Ol' Boys Roundup in May 1995 were originally part of the church-burning task force. They have since been reassigned.

That was a step in the right direction, but it will take more to allay the misgivings of Southern blacks, almost all of whom believe the fires have been set by organized hate groups. They are unmoved by Patrick's insistence that to date there is no evidence of a widespread conspiracy. Even if a vigorous, thorough investigation is taking place, it does not matter if that investigation's results are not believed by those who have lost the most in the church fires, and they won't, unless blacks also become convinced that every possibility is being seriously considered—including the alarming notion that some of the investigators are themselves compromised by racist attitudes.

One Year Later: The Family That Triumphed Over Terrorism[4]

Cartoons blare from the TV, the refrigerator door is in perpetual motion, and the kids are squabbling. "Mine, mine!" shrieks 3-year-old Rebecca Denny. Red ponytail flying, she lunges for a stuffed bear that her 4-year-old brother Brandon, has made off with. He teases her a bit longer, then surrenders the toy with a satisfied giggle. In the cozy kitchen of their Oklahoma City ranch house the children's parents Jim and Claudia Denny steal a kiss as they listen to the din. They cannot imagine a more joyful noise.

But a quick tour through this modest U-shaped house dispels any illusion that these are everyday people living ordinary lives. A framed letter from Hillary Rodham Clinton hangs on the wall over the sofa alongside a gallery of family portraits. In the front hallway, twin Congressional Medals of Valor are on display with a proclamation honoring the recipients—Brandon and Rebecca Denny. In the kids' bedroom, Claudia, 37, takes down two white firefighters' hats from a shelf. "These are special," she murmurs, reading the fire department's inscription, beneath emblems declaring Rebecca and Brandon assistant chiefs: "Even firefighters have heroes and you are ours. May God bless you."

"...Oklahoma City—the worst act of terrorism ever committed on American soil."

The Denny's already consider themselves blessed. They cling to these mementos as reminders, not of the horror they confronted last April 19, but of the compassion and love that have carried them through the darkest hours any parent can fathom. Their two children survived the bombing of the federal building in downtown Oklahoma City—the worst act of terrorism ever committed on American soil. And though Brandon and Rebecca were severely injured in the blast, they instantly became symbols of hope, in this country and abroad. Both the bedroom they share and their playroom are filled with gifts from strangers wanting to ease their pain. The plush Eiffel Tower came from Paris. A church in Sedona, AZ, sent whimsical rocking horses hand-carved by a parishioner. A hockey player with the New York Islander's gave the kids a team-autographed jersey. And a group of local hospital switchboard operators pooled their money to buy a stuffed while bunny with floppy ears. All told, the Denny's have received more than 6,000 cards and letters, some of them addressed only to "Brandon in Oklahoma City." Neither Brandon nor his sister ever asks what happened to them on that awful spring morning when a bomb claimed 169 lives. Most of Brandon and Rebecca's playmates and all of their teachers died in the explosion. But even as the anniversary passes and prosecutors prepare to bring Timothy McVeigh and Terry

---

[4]Article by Tamara Jones, from *Good Housekeeping* 222:83-5 + Ap. '96. Copyright © 1996 Tamara Jones. Reprinted with permission.

Nichols to trial for the bombing, the Denny's remain determinedly upbeat.

"After coming face-to-face with that building, there is nothing in this life or any other life that could ever scare me again," declares Jim, an energetic 51-year-old with the trademark Denny red hair. Claudia, his second wife, listens quietly, shaking her head when asked if she feels hatred for those who hurt her children. "There's no time for that," she says simply. The Denny's choose not to follow news of the investigation or trial too closely. "I'm counting on the justice system to prevail," says Claudia, who has worked most of her adult life for the federal government. Logic tells them that whoever parked the truck full of explosives beneath the building's daycare center had to have seen the baby cribs lined up along the picture windows, and most likely knew that innocent children were inside. Still, the Denny's have refused to let themselves be swept away by anger or self-pity.

"...little Rebecca feels a sense of protectiveness toward her brother, chasing off strangers who approach his wheelchair..."

"Out of bad, there always comes something good," Jim says now. He repeats the words like a mantra. "The most important thing for people to know is this: From the time we found Brandon, everything for us has been a positive."

But there's no denying that the bombing has become a reference point in their lives. *Before* and *after* crop up frequently in conversation. Before, Brandon loved to run and could clearly enunciate words like *hippopotamus*. After, a small wheelchair is parked in the dining room, and every little word he utters—*ball, bye, dog*—is a victory. He's had six operations on his brain, and beneath his sandy hair, his skull is indented on one side where doctors had to remove damaged tissue. A shunt implanted on the other side helps fight off dangerous infections. As with any patient who has suffered brain trauma, Brandon's long-term prognosis is unknown. But his parents dismiss any doubts.

"Brandon will be back," Claudia says firmly. "I feel it down inside my heart...I just know that." She schedules her week around his various therapy sessions—including physical therapy to build strength on his weak right side and to unclench the hand he holds in a fist, and horseback riding to rebuild his sense of balance and confidence. Progress had been slow at times, heartening at others. Jim, Claudia, and members of their extended family cheer Brandon on, literally every step of the way. When he is strong enough to walk, with someone holding him under his arms, he demands to march back and forth through the house. "Honk, honk!" he says, laughing, to anyone in his path. "Hey," Jim calls as his son stomps by, "Brandon's walkin' and Brandon's talkin'. What a cool guy!" Even little Rebecca feels a sense of protectiveness toward her brother, chasing off strangers who approach his wheelchair when the family is out in-public. "My Brandon!" she shouts.

Rebecca went home after ten days in the hospital, and the tiny scars that riddle her milky white skin are barely noticeable now. But Claudia still has to fight tears when she remembers how her baby looked when she first saw her after the bombing. Claudia felt the explosion three blocks away, where she was working as a clerk for the Internal Revenue Service. "I thought it was our building at first," she recalls. "It was filing season, and we had been threatened before." A few miles away, in the office where he manages his brother's toolmaking business, Jim heard the window blinds rattle. A native Californian, he shrugged it off, thinking it was a small earthquake.

Within minutes, though, the news bulletins came over TV and radio: explosion at the federal building. Claudia joined the crowds downtown already making their way to the building; Jim jumped in his car and raced to the scene. He remembers how his eyes automatically searched out the second floor of the building, where the day-care center had looked out onto the street. "It was gutted," he recalls. "Gone." Jim tried in vain to push past the police line. "I have two children in there," he cried. "I have to get in!" Panicked, he ran around to the back, hoping to sneak into the demolished building that way. He met up with Claudia. Police told the Denny's they should go to the Red Cross command center a few blocks away and wait.

Reluctantly, Jim and Claudia huddled with the other stunned families at the center, where they were joined by Tim, one of Jim's three grown sons from his first marriage. After about 90 minutes, a Red Cross worker pulled them aside: An unidentified little girl had been found alive and was being prepped for surgery at Integris Southwest Medical Center. She had red hair. "That's us!" Jim exulted. He and Claudia sped to the hospital, leaving Tim behind to wait for news about Brandon. Twenty-one children and three adults had been inside the newly refurbished day-care center and rescuers initially held out little hope of finding any of them alive.

At Southwest Medical Center, Rebecca was conscious but seriously injured. The left side of her tiny body, from face to foot, looked as if it had been sandblasted. Her arm and collarbone were broken. "I could not touch her," Claudia recalls, her soft voice growing softer. "There was nowhere on her body she didn't have a bruise or a cut." Rebecca would need 133 stitches above the neck alone to close the slash wounds on her face and inside her mouth, where doctors found a piece of blue plastic. The FBI now holds the fragment as evidence; investigators believe it was a chunk of the barrel used to hold the explosives that tore through Rebecca Denny's cheek. But Rebecca was alive, and the Denny's knew they had a miracle. Now they could only pray for a second one.

It came three hours later, when Tim Denny called his father from Presbyterian Hospital. There was a little boy there, gravely injured. The explosion had blown a hole the size of a quarter through the child's head. He was on life-support systems. His features were so bloody and swollen through the swath of bandages that Tim could not even say for sure whether it was his baby brother. "Just go, just go, just go!" Claudia urged Jim. He left his wife with Rebecca and hurried across town to the other hospital. His heart ached at the sight of the motionless boy hooked up to all those machines.

Tenderly, Jim went to check the inside of the child's left thigh. He found a tiny pink birthmark in the shape of a kitten's paw print. It was the only way he knew this was his son.

Doctors, nurses, and other workers at both hospitals became surrogate family for the Denny's as they endured the excruciating scouring of Rebecca's wounds, and prayed that Brandon's life-threatening infections would subside. Hospital staffers were so eager to follow the boy's progress that ICU nurse Carlene Anteau created a "Brandon Update" newsletter in the hospital computer system. Family members, including Jim's older sons and Claudia's father, took turns keeping watch in the children's rooms. There was only one rule: Never let them see you cry. "If anyone looked like they couldn't handle it or were going to lose it, we got them out of there," Jim says. At Brandon's bedside, Jim talked incessantly to his unconscious son, prattling on about baseball games they would play, or about Brandon's beloved Mighty Morphin' Power Rangers. As days stretched into weeks, a rocking chair was put in Brandon's room, and nurses would peek in to find Jim cradling his unresponsive child, telling him how everything was going to be all right—though doctors cautioned that even if Brandon did make it, he might never walk, talk, or feed himself again. "Jim was strong from the very first day," recalls Anteau. "We all thought he was going to have to break. But he never did."

"What seemed like a devastating setback became a blessed turning point..."

Claudia kept a similar round-the-clock vigil with Rebecca, sleeping in her room and playing cartoons continuously on the VCR, so if her daughter woke up, she wouldn't be scared. "What she went through, bless her heart," Claudia says. "It took five adults to hold her down when they scrubbed her wounds, and they did it three times a day." Claudia learned how to change dressings and insert an intravenous line so she could care for Rebecca at home after her discharge.

Brandon spent 45 days at Presbyterian and another 55 days at a rehabilitation center in Dallas before finally coming home. The Denny's celebrated in August with a trip to California to see Jim's mother and enjoy VIP tours of Disneyland, Sea World, and the Disney studios. But Brandon seemed cranky and listless. Once home, his skull suddenly swelled, and he was rushed to the emergency room. "That was the one time I got really, really angry and then bitter," Claudia says. "To have come this far..." Surgeons now found two pieces of wallboard or wood in Brandon's brain; once again, he was fighting for his life. The hospital had planned a big party to celebrate Brandon's fourth birthday. Now the "Brandon Update" reported that the party was off; the little boy was getting ready for surgery. But Jim's familiar mantra held true. What seemed like a devastating setback became a blessed turning point: It was only after this surgery that Brandon began talking again and took his first steps. Out of bad came good.

Anteau still keeps the "Brandon Update" current, and, like other hospital staff members, continues to share the family's milestones. "I never thought Brandon would get this far," she admits. When she called the Denny's in October to check in, Jim put Brandon on the phone and Anteau felt tears well up upon hearing her patient speak words for the first time.

Medical bills—more than $300,000 so far—have been covered by insurance, and a trust fund established for the family by Larry Denny, Jim's brother, offers a cushion against unexpected expenses in the future. A scholarship fund set up by Oklahoma Governor Frank Keating guarantees a college education for Rebecca, Brandon, and other children who survived the bombing and/or lost a parent. The Denny's have not sought professional counseling, though both parents still feel the effects of the trauma. Claudia finds herself overly cautious in public: "Even at the mall, I'm nervous," she admits. She has not returned to her job at the IRS; colleagues have donated their vacation and sick time so she can remain on paid leave. Jim, too, has moments of anxiety. He is working again, "but I really hate it. I just miss these guys so much, I want to be with Claudia and the kids all the time. But the bills have to be paid." His anguish comes from fear as well as love. Jim once found himself asking investigators whether Brandon and Rebecca were still in danger, whether "whoever did it would come back to finish the job."

"'When I don't feel brave,' says Jim, 'all I have to do is see how brave Brandon is.'"

The Denny's do not stay in touch on a regular basis with the other families from the day-care center, though the mother of two toddlers killed in the bombing came by recently to give Brandon a favorite toy that had belonged to his little friend. "We don't know what to say to these people whose children were lost," Jim reflects. The Denny's also struggle with the feeling that they somehow let their own children down, and Claudia insists she'll never leave her children in day-care again.

Still, the Dennys have overcome most of their fears and doubts. "When I don't feel brave," says Jim, "all I have to do is see how brave Brandon is. He never gripes, never complains." In the hospital, Jim had told Claudia, "If we can get Brandon and Rebecca home and sitting in front of the TV, I'll watch *The Lion King* another 365 times." It's a promise he's happily kept. And watching Jim and Rebecca sing the Barney song for the umpteenth time, hugging and smothering each other with kisses mid-chorus, you can understand why Jim says, "I wouldn't trade my life for anyone's in this world."

Jim returned to the Catholic Church a few years ago: after the bombing, Claudia decided to convert to Catholicism, and she's made plans to be baptized with her two miracle children. The family pastor, the Reverend Ben Zoeller, saw the Dennys' faith deepen during the crisis. "The whole time, from the very beginning, I've never seen anybody as positive as they were" he says. "I thought after two, three, maybe five weeks that they would crash and burn. But they never did."

Although experts have told the Dennys that their children can't remember what happened on that day in April, Jim and Claudia know otherwise. "You can't lay Brandon flat on his back or he starts screaming," his father says. "We still don't know where the kids were found or who pulled them out, but I will bet you anything they found Brandon on his back." He is equally convinced that Brandon and Rebecca have flashbacks to that horrific morning and are simply too young to articulate them. In her sleep, Rebecca sometimes calls out for Brandon and for her day-care teacher killed in the bombing. And when a fierce thunderstorm passed over Oklahoma City at three o'clock one morning, Brandon bolted upright in bed. I never heard him scream like that," Jim recalls with a shudder. "That was the blast. I know they remember it. I wish they didn't."

Someday, when Brandon and Rebecca are older, Jim and Claudia will tell them about the bombing. "I'm not going to hide it from them," says Claudia. She and Jim will explain that there are some bad people in the world, who do bad things. But then they will show their children the toys and tell them about the strangers who prayed for them, about the doctors and nurses who saved them, and carried them from the rubble. What they will say is that the world is filled with good people, too.

IV. Preventive Measures

Editor's Introduction

Considering the magnitude of a terrorist event, i.e. the sheer number of people indirectly or directly affected, it is no surprise that such events become the focus of federal attention. The last section of this *Reference Shelf* volume discusses the various plans for countering acts of terrorism. Central to all of the articles is the realization that advances in technology are likely to increase the severity of terrorist attacks. Yet despite this alarming prospect, the measures taken to prevent terrorist attacks must take into account the civil liberties of American citizens, the vast majority of whom do not commit terrorist actions.

The first article, "A Dangerous Future," by Robert Kupperman, Senior Advisor for the Center for Strategic and International Studies, writing in the *Harvard International Review*, evaluates the destructive potential of criminal arsenals. Kupperman notes that "the United States must be prepared to cope with domestic terrorist attacks far more severe than the World Trade Center bombing." High-tech weapons and the stockpiling of arms, according to Kupperman, may lead terrorism to "take on new, devastating forms," and all subsequent policy must reflect this reality.

"Terrorizing the Constitution," by David Cole, writing in *The Nation,* examines the antiterrorism bills and raises the question of whether it is necessary to alter the Constitutional balance between governmental power and personal freedom. Cole asserts that it is common for terrorist prevention plans to restrict Constitutional rights without achieving any net reduction in terrorist violence.

Eugene H. Methvin, writing in the *National Review,* anaylzes the often-raised conflict between civil liberties and security. He cites ways in which public rights may be infringed by new and stricter measures designed to protect the country against terrorism, but argues that despite these infringements there must be a higher level of federal surveillance if terrorism is to be effectively controlled.

The last article in this volume, "What Can Be Done About Terrorism," is written by Louis J. Freeh, the director of the FBI. Freeh lists terrorist events, in the U.S. and abroad, and theorizes that all terrorism is "fueled by extreme hatred." Asking for broader powers for the FBI, Freeh states that the Bureau has no interest in the ideologies and politics of dissident groups per se, and is only concerned with prevention of actual terrorist attacks. Included in this article is a brief summary of the history of the FBI's involvement with counterterrorism.

A Dangerous Future[1]

The Destructive Potential of Criminal Arsenals

Twenty years ago, the first debates about terrorist weapons and objectives took form in the United States. Focusing on counterterrorist strategies, the Central Intelligence Agency and the Departments of State, Defense, and Energy fought over bureaucratic leadership while authority within the Federal Bureau of Investigation (FBI) was divided internally between the Hoover-bureau model and the FBI Academy. The Academy led much of the intellectual debate, an exception to its previously less influential character. Overall, the FBI led the fight against domestic terrorism while the Cabinet Committee to Combat Terrorism working group became the interagency leader in coping with terrorism abroad. Among the members of the US counterterrorism community, there existed a tense atmosphere of fear when terrorist incidents occurred and boredom when they did not.

Brian Jenkins, then of the Rand Corporation, dominated the debate over counterterrorism within the social sciences. As the then-Chief Scientist of the US Arms Control and Disarmament Agency (ACDA), I became the unofficial government spokesperson for anticipating high-tech attacks. Potential assaults under my purview at the ACDA included both the use of agents of mass destruction and attacks on the nation's infrastructure. Over the years, Jenkins and I largely assumed adversarial roles when, in retrospect, our opinions concerning the future of terrorism were probably not highly dissimilar. Despite our agreements, the assumed difference of opinion between us focused the emerging debate over terrorism and served as a catalyst in polarizing views about terrorism both in the United States and internationally.

"Enforcement agencies will face greater challenges as they attempt to understand and effectively confront the terrorism and organized crime of the future."

Given advances in technology and the increased availability of weapons of mass destruction, it is time to reassess terrorism. The geopolitics of global criminality have changed rapidly during the past two decades, granting tomorrow's criminals access to vast information bases and weaponry. Consequently, law enforcement has become an essential part of any comprehensive national security strategy. Enforcement agencies will face greater challenges as they attempt to understand and effectively confront the terrorism and organized crime of the future. Crime will be sophisticated and possibly subtle, and the United States must be prepared to cope with domestic terrorist attacks far more severe than the World Trade Center bombing. With the world changing in ever more dangerous ways—and becoming ever more threatened by unconventional terrorist attacks—now is the time to think ahead.

[1]Article by Robert Kupperman, Senior Advisor to the Center for Strategic and International Studies, former Chief Scientist of the Arms Control and Disarmament Agency, from *Harvard International Review* 17:46 Je. 1, '95. Copyright © 1995 by *Harvard International Review*. Reprinted with permission.

Different Assessments

In a 1993 speech before a Department of Defense audience, Jenkins acknowledged that forecasting terrorism was largely speculative. Having offered this caution and noting the decline of superpower competition and the spread of anti-American sentiments, he then made a number of conservative predictions. There would be little technological change in terrorist tactics, he stated, although some might use more standoff weaponry and command-detonated bombs. Without fear of self-contradiction, Jenkins then suggested that terrorists may use nuclear, radiological, chemical, or biological weapons and computer viruses. But he claimed that even if terrorists were to use chemical attacks, they could design them to prevent mass casualties. Furthermore, terrorists have yet to attack well-defended or truly high-tech targets, or attempt to penetrate computers or employ poisons or toxic chemicals. Jenkins concluded that terrorism overall will persist. He argued that Middle Eastern terrorism will remain the greatest threat, that terrorist spill-over from guerrilla wars will continue but not lead to major crises, and that terrorist activities in Western Europe will taper off. He predicted new sources of violence in the Balkans, the former Soviet Union, and Asia as well as new threats to the United States from narcotics traffickers, North Korean operatives, Islamic extremists, and issue-oriented extremists. Finally, Jenkins argued that while high-casualty terrorist strikes are possible, the current scattered and low-casualty character of terrorist operations would not change dramatically, and that mass destruction terrorism is highly unlikely.

While I largely agree with Jenkins, more so now than in the past, I fear that terrorism can unexpectedly take on new, devastating forms. Jenkins is probably correct that terrorism will not change radically, but the consequences of his being wrong are too great to risk. Thus, Jenkins and I part company regarding the degree of the threat. Jenkins, moreover, does not adequately address several policy and operational problems. First, if, for example, terrorists do go high-tech, no government agency currently exists to cope with the repercussions of their attack. The physical and psychological costs of such a major high-tech offensive in the United States could prove overwhelming. In this context, it is important to note the tacit assumption that terrorists are incapable of seriously miscalculating the consequences of their attack. Second, many seasoned observers and federal law enforcement officials assume that an unstated agreement exists between the West and terrorist-sponsoring nations, such as Iran and Syria. This understanding holds that state-sponsors will restrain terrorists from engaging in massive attacks, leaving their attacks as little more than annoyances. Yet this view fails to acknowledge that had the World Trade Center bombing been better designed, thousands could have died and the US financial community could have come to a grinding halt. Several of the terrorists captured were planning attacks of monumental proportions—Manhattan would have been severely damaged.

Future security is increasingly threatened as terrorism becomes enmeshed in the fabric of global organized crime. The growing global interconnectivity of organized crime—with its vast resources and its ability to move money, share information, exploit and manipulate modem technology, and provide endless quantities of black market commodities—has forever changed the way terrorists do business. Terrorists have always sought leverage to penetrate international power and influence. A major change today is that otherwise small and insignificant terrorist groups can join with organized crime to exercise disproportionate leverage. We used to think that small groups could only execute small acts of violence. Because of the benefits accruing from these new criminal arrangements, however, this may no longer be the case. An essential question emerges as to whether terrorists are becoming transformed globally into organized criminals or are just using the funds generated by their own criminal activities to support their terrorist agendas.

"...endless quantities of black market commodities— ha[ve] forever changed the way terrorists do business."

Another troubling security issue that the world will face is the plethora of target choices available to terrorists, the most tempting of which may be infrastructural, such as the information superhighway. As information is the currency of the future, the potential exploitation of this target deserves priority consideration. Everything from currencies to stocks and bonds to corporate secrets are now stored in electronic formats. Never before has information been more accessible or susceptible to interception, contamination, or even complete deletion. Moreover, elements of the civilian, financial, intelligence, law enforcement, and military communities are becoming dependent on information transmitted electronically on the information superhighway for the daily conduct of their affairs. Information systems are vulnerable to both traditional physical threats (hard attacks) as well as to forms of soft attack, including jamming, "spoofing," hacking and over-loading electrical circuits. In 1988, for example, Robert Morris injected a malicious code dubbed "Worm" into the Internet, bringing the entire system to a complete standstill. The emerging information superhighway may take on new dimensions of vulnerability in the future. The horrifying prospect of infrastructural attacks by terrorists may cause law enforcement agencies to simply throw up their hands. Technological interconnections have become so integral to our lives as to be virtually invisible. Deliberately targeted attacks—for example, on the Public Switched Network or FedWire—could bring an industrialized society to a temporary, but lengthy, halt through the disruption of interlocking networks. A major power failure could interrupt the Internet and other computer networks, food supply chains, sanitation and water systems, fuel provision systems, and transportation systems.

Threats to the United States

The increasing aggressiveness and effectiveness of terrorist attacks became evident to the American public with the bombing of the World Trade Center on February 26, 1993. Until then, the FBI and local law enforcement had been complacent about the possibility of major acts of international terrorism occurring in the United States. Yet the bombing shocked the US government into recognizing that international terrorism is among the nation's most important law enforcement and national security challenges. Numerous challenges exist to contemporary US counterterrorist efforts. First, budget cuts, loss of expertise, and lack of focus have limited foreign counterterrorism—the first line of defense against international terrorism. International cooperation, an effective and necessary method of deterring terrorism, has all too often been treated as a minor political function in the Department of State. Second, local law enforcement units are poorly trained to detect and deter terrorism. Overreaction can lead to the violation of human rights and the alienation that leads to political violence. The Immigration and Naturalization Service (INS) is overwhelmed, under-trained, and unprepared to regulate legal immigration or to track illegal immigrants who enter the United States. The Federal Emergency Management Agency (FEMA), responsible for confronting the consequences of terrorist attacks, is incapable of rapid and effective response.

"...with the bombing of the World Trade Center, a psychological barrier of security has been breached by the terrorists."

Although the United States was a target for international terrorist activities, including bombing and hostage-taking, throughout the 1980s, the American mainland was never directly threatened. Americans in the Middle East and symbols of the United States abroad were more convenient and accessible targets. However, with the bombing of the World Trade Center, a psychological barrier of security has been breached by the terrorists. In New Jersey and in Brooklyn, a blind shaykh raised his voice against the government of Egypt and its supporter, the United States. He condemned the "demon" called America and exhorted his followers to "destroy their edifices." That is precisely what some of Shaykh Umar Abd'Al Rahman's disciples attempted. Although the bombing of the World Trade Center was only partially successful, the "Gang That Could Not Shoot Straight" caused several hundred million dollars of damage, more than a thousand injuries, and six deaths. All this was accomplished by relatively untrained amateurs bound by an adherence to a fanatical view of Islam and a hatred for the role of the United States as the principal supporter of Israel. Foreign elements and governments are attempting to manipulate and exploit co-religionists and co-nationals in US urban environments. In the past, groups such as Hamas and the Irish Republican Army (IRA) have used the United States strictly as an arena to raise funds for their violent activities. Now, with ethnic tensions unleashed in the aftermath of the Cold War, the United States will likely become a terrorist target to the same extent that the United Kingdom is prey to the IRA, Italy to the Mafia, Egypt to the Islamic Jihad, Colombia to the drug cartels, and Turkey to the Kurdish PKK.

Looking Toward the Future

Indeed, as ethnic tensions rise, terrorism will increase and adversely affect the United States and its allies. The United States is now at risk from both new and old sources of terrorism. Iran, Sudan, and other countries are encouraging the spread of terrorism from North Africa to North America. As technology proliferates and Middle Eastern nations accumulate funds, terrorism will be used as leverage against other states. There is also a new architecture of loosely directed terrorists and independent operators extending from South Asia to Europe, Central Asia, and North America.

The end of the Cold War has also accelerated unconventional warfare opportunities. Although the relationship between terrorist organizations and their former state sponsors threatened the United States during the Cold War, the political parameters within which terrorists were forced to operate tended to constrain rash and ill-considered terrorist attacks. Today's relationships are ambiguous at best, with political conflicts replaced by fervent religious, ethnic, and nationalistic struggles.

The essential question for counterterrorist experts is how the rising availability of weapons on the black market will affect future terrorism. While the question remains unanswered, we do know that weapons, some of them very sophisticated, are available on the black market. The states of the former Soviet Union need money, and they have a vested economic interest in supplying weapons throughout the world. These include not only unsophisticated weaponry like the AK-47, but also very sophisticated weaponry such as biological, chemical, and nuclear armaments. Small nations and aggressive terrorist groups are likely to be the happy recipients of such weapons.

"It remains unclear how and which groups are influenced by global organized crime in the aftermath of the Cold War."

Given the apparent instability of the post-Cold War world, it is important to determine the profiles of future terrorists. Although some members of militant extremist groups are college-trained and have advanced degrees in nuclear engineering and cybernetics, most terrorists are peasants with limited training and resources. Completing the picture even further, today's terrorism is global. Terrorist organizations, no longer receiving funds from their patrons, are turning to organized crime for revenue. Realizing the financial opportunities, some groups have abandoned their ideologies to become criminal organizations and are thereby able to afford more expensive and destructive weaponry. This growing nexus must be closely examined by intelligence and law enforcement agencies. It is also necessary for counterterrorist agencies to determine the demographic factors effecting terrorists today so we can predict what business as usual will be tomorrow. It remains unclear how and which groups are influenced by global organized crime in the aftermath of the Cold War. It is also unclear how and which terrorist groups will manipulate the information superhighway.

One trend, however, is clear—state-sponsored terrorism will continue to play an active role. The danger is that state sponsors, such as Iran, can now grant terrorists access to their sophisticated technology. The Iranian Revolutionary Guard is already training the Sudanese militia according to the Iranian model and supports the training of radical Islamic activists in communities scattered throughout the world. While the techniques taught include assassinations and the use of car bombs, they may also work to devise methods that will have an even greater impact, particularly in urban Western societies. While counterterrorist technical expertise in the United States has grown, so too has the professional terrorist's ability to analyze and assess opportunities for attack. Recent urban terrorist bombings in Argentina and London are indicative of the trend.

When the dust settles, both literally and figuratively, it will become clear that the World Trade Center bombing and related events were sponsored by plausibly deniable agents of foreign governments. Iran and Iraq come to mind. Of these two, Iran is the best positioned geopolitically and logistically.

It is doubtful that "amateur terrorism" will replace state-sponsored terrorism as a tool for maintaining group visibility. Although more easily executed than state-sponsored efforts, "amateur terrorism" is much more vulnerable to intelligence and police countermeasures. Such groups will not replace sophisticated organizations. They can, however, behave as temporary irritants. Over time, amateur terrorist groups of varying sophistication will emerge. But even those most capable of garnering publicity due to their viciousness are not likely to be of great strategic consequence.

The tactics of future terrorists are as difficult to discern as the profiles of future terrorists. While I agree with Jenkins that terrorist tactics in the future will most likely be the tactics of today, I believe that we will see an acceleration of innovative changes employing more advanced technology. I suspect a number of analysts, including myself, have overstated the probability of terrorists using weapons of mass destruction. What is of immediate concern, however, is that mass destruction could be caused by the use of relatively low-tech weapons against civilians and other soft targets. Had the attack on the World Trade Center been more innovative, more casualties and even greater destruction could have resulted.

The forms of terrorism we may face go beyond bombings, airplane hijacking, or hostage-taking. State-sponsored terrorists will possess far more sophisticated tools than they do presently and will be able to resolve complex logistical and communications problems. For example, multi-phase fused explosive charges are believed to have been used in the Pan Am 103 bombing. Enhanced cryptography and portable satellite links will provide terrorists with secure lines of communication. There is concern that terrorist groups are using more lethal devices, but one must remember that they have used sophisticated explosives and detonating mechanisms for years. To destroy Pan Am 103, terrorists used a small amount of the plastic explosive Semtex, which is more powerful and harder to detect than traditional explosives. The Provisional IRA has become expert in building bombs with long-delay timing devices that can be set to explode in weeks or months, rather than in hours. The IRA almost killed British Prime Minister Margaret Thatcher and her cabinet with such a bomb in 1985. And, of course, terrorist groups may also turn to biological, chemical, and radiological weapons.

Over the years, analysts of terrorism have focused on the vulnerability of our infrastructure and on the possibility of terrorist groups resorting to weapons of mass destruction. We have neglected the subtle and complex changes in international and criminal support of terrorism that will shape the coming evolution in tactics and targets. These factors are the ones which will determine how terrorists and supercriminals will make use of the information superhighway of the future, both as a tool in doing business and as a target. Indeed, the March 20, 1995, nerve gas attack in Japan's subway system highlights the fact that mass-destruction terrorism is becoming a reality. Further, the Oklahoma City bombing, ostensibly by militia members, brings terrorism right to the heartland of America. We are lucky that currently there is no "Dr. No," since a future super-terrorist is a real possibility.

Terrorizing the Constitution[2]

The Government's Anti-Terror Proposal Attacks Everyone's Fundamental Rights

April 19 is fast approaching, and Congress knows it. If we don't have an anti-terrorism law by then, the anniversary of the Oklahoma City bombing, President Clinton will be sure to let the nation know. He's already attacked the Republicans repeatedly for their "failure" to pass such a bill, and in an election year, how can he possibly resist?

Showing signs that it may bow to this pressure, the Republican-controlled House has agreed to take up the terrorism bill once again the week of March 11. Twice before, efforts to pass it have come up short, largely because of objections from a broad-based coalition of strange bedfellows—led by the American Civil Liberties Union and the National Rifle Association—who agree that the measure would unnecessarily expand government power and infringe on personal liberties. (The Senate, which acted precipitately in the wake of the Oklahoma City bombing, passed an anti-terrorism bill by a vote of 91 to 8 in June.)

> *"...terrorism has been increasingly taken up by religious groups and cults, which may be less concerned about creating mass destruction than the traditional political terrorist."*

As a matter of short-term politics, the proposed law gives Clinton a convenient way to look tough on crime, and lets him charge the Republicans with being soft on "terrorism." But the longer-term issue—one that will be with us for decades to come—is whether terrorism today requires us to alter the constitutional balance we have so long maintained between government power and personal freedom. One need only look at Israel or Great Britain to see that when the threat of terrorism strikes home, personal liberties are often sacrificed in the name of security. The anti-terrorism bill invites us to head down that road.

Proponents of expanding government power to fight terrorism, such as the Defense Department's Peter Probst, argue that the threat today is qualitatively different from that of the past, for two reasons. First, terrorism has been increasingly taken up by religious groups and cults, which may be less concerned about creating mass destruction than the traditional political terrorist. The political terrorist, the argument goes, operates within the constraints set by the goal of obtaining political support for his cause. The religious or cult terrorist, by contrast, is not looking for political support and may harbor Armageddon-like fantasies, and thus knows no bounds.

Second, technological advances have made chemical, biological and even nuclear weapons much more widely available, and have thereby democratized the ability to inflict mass destruction. Thomas Hobbes's fears about the threat we face from our neighbor

---

[2]Article by David Cole, from *The Nation* 262:11-5 Mr 25, '96. Copyright © 1996 The Nation LP. Reprinted with permission.

are heightened if our neighbor has not simply a club but a vial of pulmonary anthrax, an incredibly lethal biological agent. Therefore, the Leviathan's powers must be augmented to meet this threat.

But how rational are these fears? And even if the concerns are justified, do the controversial elements of the anti-terrorism bill, which sharply restrict constitutional freedoms, respond to them?

There are a number of reasons to be skeptical about the claim that terrorism has qualitatively changed. Terrorism is designed to provoke terror, so we should be wary of too easily falling prey to our fear. And terrorists are easily demonized, for their willingness to engage in abominable and wholly illegitimate acts means they have rejected the norms of civilized society.

Moreover, it's only "terrorism" when the other side does it, and we always believe the worst about the other side. The charge that "these people know no bounds" is nothing new, and has repeatedly been made in this country about the "other side," whether they be Native Americans, anarchists, the Japanese during World War II or Communists.

But is it really true that terrorists today know no bounds? Hamas, Hezbollah and Islamic Jihad, for example, have been engaging terrorism for many years now, yet they have strategically targeted and timed their attacks to further their political agenda. The recent series of horrific suicide bombings in Israel, for example, broke a six-month hiatus in terror attacks there and appear aimed at disrupting the peace process. According to the U.S. government's own allegations, Sheik Omar Abdel Rahman, the Egyptian cleric serving a life sentence for his role in encouraging the World Trade Center bombers, had at times discouraged terrorism because he felt it would "be bad for Muslims." Terrorists don't abide by our bounds, but we shouldn't be quick to conclude that they know no limits whatsoever.

"...as the Oklahoma City bombers demonstrated with ordinary, widely available farming chemicals, it doesn't take advanced technology to kill scores of people in a single act."

As to advances in technology, there are no doubt more ways to destroy the world today than fifty years ago, thanks largely to the arms race. But as the Oklahoma City bombers demonstrated with ordinary, widely available farming chemicals, it doesn't take advanced technology to kill scores of people in a single act. It's not clear, therefore, that technological advances have categorically increased a threat that has long been with us.

Hostage to the Law

It is easy to be swayed by dramatic incidents like the Oklahoma City bombing, but the statistics don't support the dire predictions. According to the State Department's most recent annual report on "global terrorism," international terrorism "declined worldwide" in 1994, reaching the lowest annual total in twenty-three years. In the six years prior to 1995, there were only nine international terrorist incidents in all of North America. (By contrast, during the same period in Latin America there were 821 acts of international terrorism.)

In assessing the terrorist threat, the real question is, compared to what? When Congress voted last year to lift the 55-mile-per-hour speed limit, it knowingly increased the number of Americans who will die in automobile accidents by several thousand per year, more than terrorists have ever killed in a year worldwide. More than 20,000 people are murdered in the United States every year, the vast majority by gunfire; yet Congress has never been able to enact anything more than symbolic gun-control measures. Thus, we knowingly tolerate many conditions that pose far greater risk of harm to ourselves than terrorism.

Let's assume for a moment that we do face a qualitatively different terrorist threat today. Does that mean that we must—or should—increase government power at the expense of personal freedoms? Some anti-terrorism measures are no doubt fully justified in the light of new technologies. Lethal biological, chemical and nuclear weapons should be banned. The materials necessary to produce such weapons should be strictly controlled. "Tagging" ordinary chemicals that have legitimate uses but also might be used to produce explosives, so that they are traceable, makes good sense.

But while the anti-terrorism bill includes some measures directed at the technology of destruction, its most controversial provisions are of a categorically different character. They would sharply restrict constitutional liberties in the name of the cause. These measures seem not only misguided but counterproductive.

Consider, for example, the bill's habeas corpus provisions. Habeas corpus is the only way that most criminal defendants ever get a federal hearing on their constitutional claims. It's an incredibly important stopgap, as illustrated by the fact that some 40 percent of state-imposed death penalties are reversed in federal habeas corpus proceedings for constitutional violations that the state courts overlooked. Yet under the anti-terrorism bill, federal courts would have to defer to a states court's conclusions on constitutional questions unless the state court's decision was "arbitrary" or "unreasonable." This watering down of constitutional protections applies to *all* state crimes, from fornication to shoplifting, and has no connection whatsoever to terrorist offenses, the vast majority of which are tried in federal court. It restricts constitutional rights with no net gain in the fight against terrorism.

The bill also introduces to criminal law the concept of guilt by association, a notion we tried out, with disastrous results, during the McCarthy era. The anti-Communist laws presumed that anyone working with or assisting the Communists was guilty of the party's illegal ends, even if the individual cooperated only for purposes that were legal, such as labor organizing. The injustices and excesses of that experiment ultimately led the Supreme Court to rule that where the government seeks to hold someone accountable for supporting a group, it must prove that the individual specifically intended to further the group's unlawful ends.

Under the anti-terrorism bill, the Secretary of State could designate any foreign group as "terrorist," and it would then become a crime, punishable by up to ten years in prison, to support that group's *lawful* activities. The Secretary's designation would for all practical purposes be unreviewable, because the legal standard for what qualifies a group as terrorist relies on the Secretary's judgment that the group's activities threaten our "national security," a judgment no court is likely to second-guess.

Would this provision help stem the tide of new terrorism? Perhaps, for the Secretary of State could effectively stifle aid to a given group engaged in terrorism. But it would do so at the cost of giving the federal government unchecked power to blacklist any organization it does not support. Moreover, the bill is specifically directed at humanitarian and lawful support, since support of terrorist acts is already a crime under current law. By criminalizing those who associate with a group's lawful ends, it deters precisely the people who might have some moderating influence on the group in question. And by making peaceful political association a federal crime, the bill would authorize widespread F.B.I. political spying on nonviolent domestic organizations, an authority that history shows is bound to be abused.

A third provision of the bill would allow the government to deport immigrants—both permanent residents and those here temporarily—on the strength of secret evidence that neither the immigrant nor his or her attorney would ever see. The government would be free to submit evidence behind closed doors to a judge handpicked by Chief Justice William Rehnquist, and to make secret arguments and take secret appeals outside the immigrant's presence. This provision sacrifices the most basic tenet of the American adversarial system—that the government must confront individuals with evidence it seeks to use against them. Every time the government has sought to employ such a procedure against aliens living in the United Sates, the federal courts have held that it violates due process—most recently in a unanimous Ninth Circuit Court of Appeals decision last November, which the United States declined to appeal.

The Clinton Administration argues that such a measure is needed because it sometimes has classified information that it would like to use without having to reveal the source or specific content. But the government faces this situation every day in criminal courts across the country, where it must choose between revealing the source and not using the evidence. The rule applies no matter how heinous the crime, and no matter how sensitive the information. There simply is no other way to administer a fair system of justice, because it is impossible to defend oneself against secret evidence.

There is no question that these measures violate well-established principles of freedom of association and due process. But their proponents contend that the new world order requires a rethinking of these constitutional underpinnings. "The Constitution is not a suicide pact," as Justice Arthur Goloberg once said, and as the government has not stopped quoting since. But are these constitutional sacrifices necessary? Will they save us?

Let's turn to the two claims made about the new terrorist threat.

Terrorists today know no bounds. If that's the case, it's not clear that any of these measures are likely to save us. Our best hope is that our fellow human beings will in fact be bound by the basic principles of civilized society. And one of the most important things we can do to insure that is to honor certain fundamental limits on the power of government. Empowering the state to blacklist disfavored groups, use secret evidence and violate constitutional rights without adequate judicial review plays into the hands of zealots; it also not only feeds their paranoia but makes it seem rational. At the same time, such tactics seem likely to drive the truly dangerous underground, where they will be more difficult to track.

Some say that America's open society makes it especially vulnerable to terrorist attack. But one of the principal benefits of an open society with substantial political freedoms is that it provides peaceful ways to express opposition and to work for political change. Repressive governments tend to breed rather than contain violence. The United States has been relatively free of terrorism, I believe, largely because of, not in spite of, our political freedoms.

Finally, even if it is true that technological advances have increased the threat from terrorists, they have also increased the theat from government. New technologies give the state unprecedented ability to track its citizens' every move. As Brian Jenkins, deputy chairman of Kroll Associates, a security consulting firm, has noted, "The technology for national population control is available (counterfeit-resistant identification cards, card readers with mandatory verification at every point of commercial transactions, computer programs with profiles of every citizen) but in most cases, would be regarded as Orwellian." The threat to our freedom from new technologies, in other words, is double-edged. History suggests that we ought to be at least as concerned about government abuse as about terrorists. As Justice Louis Brandeis said, "The greatest danger to liberty lurks in insidious encroachment by men of zeal, well-meaning but without understanding." The best we can do is stick to the principles that have guided us thus far, and hope that by respecting those constitutional bounds, we will set an example that others can follow.

Anti-terrorism: How Far?[3]

Last February, a former leader of the Michigan Militia, Eric Maloney, visited the FBI and warned that Timothy McVeigh and the Nichols brothers had attended a "special operations session" three months earlier where they talked about blowing up buildings. Maloney told Brian Ross, an ABC News investigative correspondent, that the FBI turned a deaf ear. "I told them that if they didn't act on this, a whole lot of people are going to get killed," Maloney said. But the FBI was not interested because "there was nothing they felt they could do."

In the shadow of the Oklahoma City bombing, the campaign to keep America safe for terrorists revived. Rescuers were still digging victims out of the rubble when liberals leaped to their pulpits to warn against reviving the FBI's "domestic spying." They thus continued a twenty-year campaign that has destroyed the nation's domestic intelligence capacity and left Americans pathetically vulnerable to atrocities like the one in Oklahoma. They have erected a false mythology about the agency's past alleged sins. Thus the *New York Times* wailed about the FBI's and CIA's "brazen violation of American freedoms" and "contempt for the Constitution."

FBI Director Louis Freeh did mount a modest defense of law enforcement's preventive role. In testimony before the Senate Judiciary Committee he complained: "For two decades the FBI has been at an extreme disadvantage with regard to domestic groups which advocate violence. We have no intelligence or background information on them until their violent talk becomes deadly action. ...I do not support broad and undefined intelligence collection efforts—but...the first rule of self-defense is to know the enemy who intends to destroy you. Intelligence...helps to protect the American people. It should not be considered a 'dirty word.'"

"In 1971, the American Civil Liberties Union announced that 'dissolution of the nation's vast surveillance network' would henceforth be a top priority."

Enemy Within

But a dirty word it is today. In the 1970s the nation allowed its domestic anti-terrorism apparatus to be crippled and virtually disbanded. Leading the destruction was a coalition of conscientious civil libertarians and radical revolutionaries dedicated to destroying constitutional government in the United States.

In 1971, the American Civil Liberties Union announced that "dissolution of the nation's vast surveillance network" would henceforth be a top priority. It launched a "police surveillance project" headed by Yale Law Professor Frank J. Donner, identified in sworn testimony by three witnesses as a steadfast member of the Communist Party in its worst Stalinist days. The National Lawyers Guild, whose president declared its goal was "to keep the road clear

---

[3]Article by Eugene H. Methvin, senior editor *Reader's Digest*, from *National Review* 47:32 Jl 10, '95. Copyright © 1995 NATIONAL REVIEW, Inc. Reprinted with permission.

of legal roadblocks" for revolutionaries, filed lawsuits wholesale against local police intelligence units, crippling them or destroying them altogether. Old Left lawyer William Kunstler once boasted, "I stay in this profession only because I want to be a double agent, to destroy the whole...system."

The *Washington Post* and *New York Times* aided these crusades in both news and editorial columns. On December 22, 1974, the *Times* launched a major "expose" of the sins of American intelligence agencies on the domestic front. This "scoop" was based on an internal study of the CIA ordered by Director William Colby, in which subordinates were instructed to review the agency's 25-year history and report every activity that might have violated a domestic law. Colby naively handed the study over to *Times* reporter Seymour Hersh, and the newspaper treated it as a major scandal.

The U.S. Senate, meanwhile, created a select committee under the chairmanship of Frank Church (D., Idaho), the Senate's most intense left-wing ideologue. In March 1976, after more than a year of bombardment by Church and others on Capitol Hill, Attorney General Edward Levi, trying to position the weak Ford Administration for the approaching election, imposed "guidelines" on the FBI prohibiting any investigation without "specific articulable facts giving reason to believe that an individual or a group is or may be engaged in" criminal activities.

This requirement for a "criminal predicate" totally abandoned law enforcement's preventive and peace-keeping functions. In the words of one jurist, "It means every terrorist gets one free blast." Five days before Levi issued his guidelines, the FBI's intelligence division had 4,868 domestic security investigations going. Six months later there were 626. By August 1982 Congress found the number had dwindled to 38.

The high cost of this destruction of domestic intelligence was demonstrated exactly a year after Attorney General Levi issued his guidelines. In Washington, D.C., a black Muslim guru named Hamaas Abdul Khaalis and 11 followers, wielding guns and machetes, seized hostages in the B'nai B'rith headquarters, the Muslim Mosque and Cultural Center, and the District of Columbia Building—Washington's "city hall." The Hanafi Muslims (as the cult called itself) killed one person and crippled another for life in their violent takeover. The siege lasted two days before the 137 hostages were released. The Metropolitan Police Department revealed that it had withdrawn an informant from the Hanafi Muslims and destroyed their file, in response to pressure from the ACLU and other police baiters. The Senate Subcommittee on Criminal Laws and Procedures in a 1978 report asserted that if the police had had an informer in the Hanafi ranks, "the chances are 100 to 1 that they would have had intelligence enabling them to take preventive action."

It was a different story in Maryland in 1978. State Police Sergeant John Cook infiltrated the Ku Klux Klan and fed the FBI reports on its violent plottings. The FBI opened a preliminary investigation under the Levi guidelines, but closed it when nothing had happened in 90 days, as the guidelines mandated. Fortunately, the Maryland State Police did not follow the FBI's lead. They kept Sergeant Cook in place, and he worked his way into a ten-man Klan "death squad." Eventually the Klan attempted a series of bombings, including one at the home of a black congressman, Parren Mitchell. The night of their planned attacks Sergeant Cook had the pleasure of arresting them.

Terror Network U.S.A.

On October 20, 1981, in Nyack, N.Y., a dozen Black Liberation Army and Weather Underground terrorists killed a Brink's guard, wounded two others, and made away with $1.6 million. At a police barricade five miles away they killed two cops and wounded a third. Four of the robbers were captured and the cash recovered, but eight or more escaped.

"...the FBI's informants in political-terrorist groups had been cut from 1,100 to fewer than 50."

Tracing auto tags noted by witnesses, the FBI found several terrorist lairs. Seized documents showed the group was moving to a more vicious level of urban guerrilla warfare. A list profiled two dozen corporate executives and contained biographies, photos, and daily schedules of top New York and New Jersey police officials. Plots for bombings and ambush murders were evident in hand-drawn floor plans and photos of police stations and barracks. The terrorists also had a file on former President Nixon's residences. The evidence revealed a nationwide alliance of radical groups: the BLA, the Weather Underground, the separatist Republic of New Afrika, the Puerto Rican FALN. They even had links to radical feminists who ran a remote California commune where Sara Jane Moore engaged in target practice before her 1975 attempt to kill President Ford, and where the Symbionese Liberation Army kidnappers prepared their abduction of Patty Hearst and their murder of Oakland's black school superintendent, Marcus Foster. The allies had pulled off at least 18 "armed expropriations" with more than a million dollars in loot, and had freed notorious terrorists from prison. Incredibly, this Terror Network U.S.A. had operated for over five years without either police or FBI intelligence catching a hint of the connections. In those five years the FBI's informants in political-terrorist groups had been cut from 1,100 to fewer than 50, and its domestic security investigations from 20,868 to only 10 groups and 47 individuals.

The FBI had followed the Weather Underground from its beginning, when it spun off from the Students for a Democratic Society in 1969. The investigation continued after the 1976 Levi guidelines because the Weather terrorists had committed numerous bombings—including at the U.S. Capitol, the Pentagon, and some 18 other targets—prior to March 1974. But in October 1981 an FBI official admitted that "federal intelligence reports" were dropped in 1979 because the Weather gang "has not been active since it claimed responsibility for the 1977 bombing of a federal building in Seattle."

So unless a terrorist network announces itself periodically with press releases claiming credit for its bombings, the FBI will not chase it? That was the practice if not the disclosed rule—and continues almost so today. And the G-Men had good reasons to drop their pursuit of the Weather terrorists. Incredibly, the Carter Justice Department had more than two dozen lawyers and a grand jury investigating 132 FBI agents for alleged civil-rights violations of relatives and friends of fugitive terrorists, while none pursued the terrorists themselves.

In 1988, the anti-intelligence combine battered the FBI again just to keep the watchdogs intimidated. The Center for Constitutional Rights, founded in 1966 by Kunstler and three other Old Left lawyers, used the Freedom of Information Act to obtain from the FBI some 1,200 pages of files on the Committee in Solidarity with the People of El Salvador (CISPES).

The *New York Times* and *Washington Post* promptly disseminated the FBI's outrages. "FBI agents took photographs of marchers and recorded their automobile license numbers," *Times* reporter Philip Shenon panted. "Agents were also authorized to begin surveillance of students at Florida State University." And the *Post*'s Howard Kurtz seemed slack-jawed that "FBI agents investigated nuns, union members, and college students; checked up on church forums and Knights of Columbus dinners; photographed protestors at peaceful rallies; and distributed what they deemed offending articles from student newspapers and *People* magazine." Neither the *Post* nor the *Times* gave its readers any hint of what had triggered the FBI probe—evidence indicating that CISPES militants might be sheltering the terrorists who had perpetrated the November 7, 1983, bombing of the U.S. Capitol.

Leon Trotsky, founder of the Red Army and one of the twentieth century's chief theoreticians and proponents of terrorism, proclaimed, "No terrorist group can function without a screen of sympathizers." CISPES clearly fit the definition of a terrorist screen. In May 1980 Fidel Castro ordered the various Marxist paramilitary factions warring against the Salvadoran government to form a unified command as the condition for greater East Bloc support. The new umbrella organizations—the military Farabundo Marti National Liberation Front (FMNL) and its political/diplomatic arm, the Revolutionary Democratic Front (FDR)—launched a program to build support inside the United States. Shortly thereafter, conventions of leftists were held in Los Angeles and Washington, and CISPES was born.

In 1983 the FBI learned that individuals in contact with the FDR/FMLN planned to establish clandestine cells in the United States to commit murders, sabotage, and bank robberies in support of the Salvadoran guerrillas. On March 30 Headquarters authorized 11 field offices to investigate CISPES locally. Within a month, a bomb had exploded at the National War College in Washington, D.C. Numerous bombings followed—including the one at the U.S. Capitol—and anonymous "communiques" proclaimed solidarity with the Salvadoran insurgents.

CISPES members were the prime suspects until late March 1984. Then the FBI learned that some of the Nyack fugitives and their allies were responsible. However, as a result of its investigation, the FBI was able to head off the disruptive demonstrations CISPES was planning at the GOP convention in Dallas. The FBI continued its investigation until June 1985.

The entire CISPES investigation involved the equivalent of five full-time agents working over two years, and cost little more than $800,000. After the *Times* and *Post* horripilations the Justice Department's Office of Professional Responsibility and the FBI's inspection division spent almost that much investigating the CISPES investigation in order to mollify the Kunstlerites, the *Times*, the *Post*, and their congressional claque. The Senate Intelligence Committee faulted the Bureau for investigating the whole CISPES organization instead of a few specific suspects. But how was the FBI to know who the suspects were, or how extensive their network was, without looking? And who can say what mischief or mayhem the surveillance prevented—thereby coincidentally protecting the constitutional rights of the large majority of CISPES members to protest peacefully?

> *"Such movements contain only a few who will build and plant bombs, or lay and execute ambushes."*

The current criminal-conduct-only guidelines ignore the well-documented sociology of terrorist movements. Such movements contain only a few who will build and plant bombs, or lay and execute ambushes. But many will give the actors support: medical help, money, hiding places, intelligence, and such. These support networks must be built in advance of the onslaught. Building them requires words to attract and recruit sympathizers. This is the stage at which prevention is possible; and if prevention fails, swift apprehension can limit the damage.

Thus in June 1970 an FBI informant within the Black Panther Party warned of a planned ambush on Detroit police, and named the designated attackers. On the appointed day two snipers riddled a police cruiser with armor-piercing bullets. Miraculously the two officers were only wounded. The killers were intercepted when they returned to their residence, and sent away for long prison terms. Three other named Panthers scouting another section of Detroit for a diversionary target were caught with illegal weapons and sent to jail as well.

Breaching the Screen

Penetrating the terrorist's screen of sympathizers requires intelligence of a surgical precision that can be obtained only with the full arsenal of clandestine operations: informant networks, electronic surveillance, covert action. An enlightening example is the first conviction under the Biological Weapons Anti-Terrorism Act of 1989.

On May 20, 1992, Colette Baker walked into the Pope County Sheriff' s Office in Glenwood, Minnesota, and complained that her husband, Doug Baker, had pointed a shotgun at her and threatened to kill her. She wanted to leave him, she said, but feared he would kill her or her parents with a powerful poison that he had bragged of possessing. To persuade the skeptical cops, the next day Mrs. Baker brought in a coffee can containing a baby-food jar, a finger-nail-polish bottle, a pair of rubber gloves, and a hand-printed note that read:

> "DOUG, Be extremely careful! After you mix the powder with the gel, the slightest contact will kill you! If you breathe the powder or get it in your eyes, you're a dead man. Dispose all instruments used. Always wear rubber gloves and then destroy them also.
>
> "Good hunting!!
>
> "P.S. Destroy this note!!"

A "smiley face" had been drawn next to the words, "Good hunting!!"

The FBI laboratory in Washington, D.C., found that the baby-food jar contained 0.7 gram of a castor-bean extract known as ricin, the third most deadly poison known. This tiny amount was enough to kill more than 100 people. Ricin has no antidote and is virtually impossible to detect in post-mortem analysis. (Ricin was the poison the KGB-controlled Bulgarian secret service used to murder Georgi Markov on a London street in 1978.)

The second bottle in Mrs. Baker's can contained a common skin-care product impregnated with dimethyl sulfoxide (DMSO), a powerful solvent that can transport toxic substances through the skin into the bloodstream in seconds.

This laboratory analysis was enough to get the FBI's concentrated attention. For more than a year local police had been passing along tipsters' warnings about a shadowy group of tax protestors called the Patriots Council, meeting sporadically in various central-Minnesota towns such as St. Cloud, Alexandria, Glenwood, and Starbuck. The group met on Sundays under guise of discussing religion, but there was hot talk against lawmen. One informant named three acquaintances who had discussed procuring assault rifles, killing a sheriff's deputy, and blowing up a federal building.

The FBI knew ricin was a favorite item in the paranoid press. One sheet, published in Oregon, advertised ricin as the "Silent Tool of Justice...agent of choice for CIA, KGB, etc. A single bean will kill an evildoer." Mrs. Baker's coffee can was just the lucky break the FBI needed to prevent what might have been a deadly disaster. This was preventive law enforcement at its best. The FBI went back to the sheriff's detectives who had been reporting on the Patriots Council and recruited one of the tipsters, Scott Loverink, as an informant. Over the next 14 months Loverink had more than one hundred contacts with the plotters. They had ordered the instructions from Oregon, grown the castor beans, extracted the ricin, and were trying to decide how to use it. IRS agents, U.S. marshalls, and local sheriff's deputies were suggested targets.

Last August, the FBI arrested Doug Baker and LeRoy Wheeler, who grew the castor beans and whose fingerprints were on the coffee can and rubber gloves. On February 28 of this year, a federal jury convicted them of possessing a biological toxin intended for use as a weapon. Meanwhile the Oregon man who ran "Maynard's Avenging Angel Supply" mail-order business was sent to prison on weapons violations. Had it not been for Doug Baker's indiscretion in pointing a shotgun at his wife, and her delivery of the ricin stash to the police, biological terrorism might have erupted in the United States well ahead of the sarin-gas murders in Tokyo's subway system.

In the wake of the Oklahoma City bombing, Kunstler's CCR struck again. This time it used the Freedom of Information Act to obtain 22 of 199 pages from FBI files on ACT-UP, the militant AIDS activist group. The files showed that, in 1990–91, when the group had scheduled protests at the U.S. Capitol and National Institutes of Health, tipsters told the FBI that some members planned violence to attract media attention. The FBI passed along the tips to relevant law-enforcement agencies and like any good bureaucracy filed them, but did no independent investigation.

But the *Times* and the *Post* once again ran accusatory stories about FBI domestic spying. Steven Michael, chairman of the ACT-UP Washington office, demanded a congressional investigation and told the Post, "They are caught with their hand in the cookie jar. I really genuinely believe that this was politically motivated. Their response is to spy on us. I don't feel safe, I don't feel comfortable. The mere fact that the FBI has a file on my organization frightens me. We have never committed an act of violence. They have no basis to even have page one."

Thus the campaign to make America safe for terrorists continues. Let the buyer beware.

What Can Be Done About Terrorism?[4]

Hundreds of special agents have been assigned to the FBI's Counterterrorism Program and legal attaches are working with foreign law enforcement officials to combat, respectively, domestic and overseas-based threats against Americans.

The bombing of the Murrah Federal Building in Oklahoma City brought terrorism to the nation's heartland. It also brought terrorism into countless living rooms across the nation—with images so graphic they shall not, indeed can not, be forgotten. This was another example of the immense suffering Americans have endured at the hands of terrorists:

- April, 1983: The U.S. Embassy in Beirut, Lebanon, was bombed, leaving 16 dead and more than 100 injured.
- October, 1983: The U.S. Marine barracks in Beirut was bombed, resulting in 241 deaths.
- June, 1985: TWA Flight 847 was hijacked. U.S. Navy diver Robert Stethem, who was on board, was brutally murdered, his body dumped on the airport tarmac.
- February, 1988: Marine Lt. Col. William Higgins—part of the United Nations peacekeeping force in Lebanon—was kidnapped and later murdered.
- December, 1988: Pan Am Flight 103 was blown up over Lockerbie, Scotland, with 270 killed.
- February, 1993: New York City's World Trade Center was bombed by Islamic extremists, leaving six dead and hundreds injured.
- March, 1995: American diplomatic personnel were murdered in a hail of machine gun fire on the streets of Karachi, Pakistan.

Terrorists also perpetrated the murder of athletes at the 1972 Munich Summer Olympics, bombings in Buenos Aires, Paris, and London, and poison gas attacks in Tokyo's subway system.

Although there are different types of terrorism, one common thread in all of these dreadful crimes is that the innocent suffer. Too many Americans have been victimized by terrorists, in the U.S. and other countries.

It is essential that terrorism be viewed in broad terms. Inevitably, it is fueled by extreme hatred. Those who harbor such hatred live in a world that is colored by bigotry, shaded by conspiracy, and framed by ignorance. Some claim there are plots to take control of the world's financial markets and the mass media and to surrender

---

[4]Article by Louis J. Freeh, Director, FBI, Washington, DC, from *USA Today Magazine* 124:24 Ja 1, '96. Copyright © 1996 USA Today Magazine. Reprinted with permission.

the U.S. to foreign military control. Others direct their ire at corporate America and evolving technology. Paranoia drives some to lash out at anyone unlike themselves.

Take the Unabomber suspect, for example. This self-described terrorist, who is responsible for murdering three persons and injuring 23 others, followed up his most recent mail bomb with a letter to *The New York Times*. In it, he said that he killed a business executive in December, 1994, because Thomas Mosser worked for a company whose "business is the development of techniques for manipulating people's attitudes." In that same letter, the bomber wrote: "The people we are out to get are the scientists and engineers, especially in critical fields like computers and genetics." Among the Unabomber's stated goals is "the destruction of the worldwide industrial system." Lengthy excerpts of his manifesto were published in the *Washington Post* and *The New York Times* on Aug. 1, 1995, followed by a 35,000-word manuscript in the Post on Sept. 19, when he promised to cease the bombings if they printed both. It remains to be seen if he will keep his word. [He was identified as Theodore Kaczynski and arrested.]

Bold steps are needed to combat terrorists—and the FBI is taking them. For instance, we committed every necessary resource in order to resolve fully the deadly bombing in Oklahoma City, just as we did in New York City, when the World Trade Center was bombed in February, 1993. I have strengthened the FBI's Counterterrorism Program by re-assigning hundreds of special agents to investigate these offenses. However, we need more investigative tools to improve the ability of the U.S. to respond to the terrorist threat. At the same time, I recognize that these tools must be used carefully and must preserve the individual liberties and constitutional rights that are so essential in our democracy.

"We all are bound by the Constitution, due process considerations, and the American legal system."

In this regard, I applaud the leadership that Pres. Clinton and Attorney General Janet Reno have shown. They understand that—consistent with America's democratic traditions—more must be done to fight terrorists. Thus, the President has proposed specific steps to be taken—including resource and personnel enhancements. Just as in a time of war, both political parties have agreed to put aside partisan differences while considering those measures.

The FBI is not seeking broad and undefined intelligence collection abilities. Nevertheless, law enforcement agencies have to know as much as possible about those individuals and groups that are advocating deadly violence in furtherance of their causes.

I do not urge investigative activity against persons or groups exercising their legitimate constitutional rights. Nor do I suggest that we should target people who simply disagree with our government. We all are bound by the Constitution, due process considerations, and the American legal system. Each of them protects the American people and those who serve in law enforcement.

The FBI is not looking to investigate lawful activity. It is not concerned about people or groups because of their ideology or philosophy. As I testified before Congress in April, 1995, "We do not need the business. The FBI has lots of important work to do in protecting the people and the United States."

The FBI's involvement in counterterrorism is not something new. It dates back to 1982, when Pres. Ronald Reagan designated the FBI as the lead agency for countering terrorism in the U.S. Those responsibilities further were expanded in 1984 and 1986, when Congress passed laws giving the FBI authority to investigate crimes of terrorism abroad against Americans, such as murder and hostage-taking.

The FBI's counterterrorism mission is fairly simple to state, but perhaps not so easy to carry out. It is to prevent acts of terrorism before they occur and/or react to them after they occur by bringing the perpetrators to justice.

Court-authorized wiretaps are one means that law enforcement agencies use to prevent crimes from occurring. In this connection, encryption capabilities available to terrorists and other criminals endanger the future usefulness of court-authorized wiretaps. If law enforcement is to do its job effectively, this issue must be resolved.

Law enforcement agencies have another acute technological need. They must have the ability to communicate rapidly by radio and other forms of wireless communications. Local, state, and Federal law enforcement officers and agencies must be able to talk among themselves, so that a state trooper patrolling America's highways in any state has the full benefit of law enforcement's knowledge when he approaches a car with a suspect in it.

Prevention means that, through investigation, we get there before the bomb goes off, before the plane is hijacked, before innocent Americans lose their lives. This is our number-one priority.

Reaction is the law enforcement response after the fact. Although it has been over seven years since the bombing of Pan Am Flight 103, the perpetrators still have not been brought to justice. The U.S. government has not forgotten the case, though. On Nov. 14, 1991, the Department of Justice obtained indictments against the two Libyan intelligence operatives allegedly responsible for the bombing—Lamen Khalifa Fhimah and Abdel Basset Ali Al-Megrahi.

Since the bombing, the UN has issued several resolutions in an attempt to force Libya to end its sponsorship of terrorism, accept responsibility for the Pan Am 103 bombing, and extradite Fhimah and Megrahi to either the U.S. or the United Kingdom to stand trial.

In March, 1995, Fhimah and Megrahi were added to the FBI's Ten Most Wanted Fugitives List. The same day, the State Department allocated up to $4,000,000 of reward money for information leading to their arrest.

There is a need for adoption of tougher worldwide anti-terrorism measures. The FBI works closely with many of its counterparts around the globe. We have found them eager to join in this common battle. Currently, the FBI has 23 legal attaches overseas—FBI agents working hand in hand with law enforcement officials from the host nations to address the growing, joint problems of terrorism and other international crimes. These agents are the U.S.'s first line

"...the State Department allocated up to $4,000,000 of reward money for information leading to their arrest."

of law enforcement defense overseas. To combat the many and varying forms of terrorism, the FBI needs more legal attaches in other nations around the world to investigate jointly and control these types of criminal acts.

All of the FBI's overseas counterterrorism investigations are conducted in close coordination with the U.S. Department of State and with the approval and support of the foreign countries where the terrorist incidents occur or may develop. For example, when Pan Am Flight 103 exploded over Lockerbie, Scotland, the FBI didn't just take over the criminal investigation. We were asked by the British and Scottish authorities to participate, and our activities abroad closely were coordinated with the State Department.

In April, 1995, under the FBI's leadership, the International Law Enforcement Academy opened in Budapest, Hungary. There, law enforcement officials from 22 nations throughout Central and Eastern Europe and the countries of the former Soviet Union will receive training in a wide variety of matters. Through the Academy, law enforcement around the world will expand its network, thereby enhancing the ability to combat—consistent with the rule of law—those who would engage in terrorism.

Law enforcement agencies can and must do everything within their power to prevent terrorist incidents from occurring. Where prevention programs fail, as they sometimes do, we must do our very best to apprehend and convict the terrorists—to see that justice is served. We owe it to the memories of their victims.

Bibliography

Books and Pamphlets

Antokol, Norman; Nudell, Mayer. No one a neutral. Alpha of Ohio '90.

Arnold, Terrell E. The violence formula. Lexington '88.

Bean, Harold G. Diplomats and terrorists II. Georgetown Univ. Inst. for the Study of Diplomacy '87.

Beres, Louis Rene. Terrorism and global security. Westview '87.

Bushnell, P. Timothy. State organized terror. Westview '91.

Cassese, Antonio. Terrorism, politics, and law; the Achille Lauro affair. Princeton Univ. Press '89.

Chaliand, Gerard. Terrorism. Saqi '87.

Charters, David. Democratic responses to international terrorism. Transnational '91.

Chomsky, Noam. Pirates & emperors. Black Rose '91.

Clutterbuck, Richard L. Terrorism in an unstable world. Routledge '94.

Clutterbuck, Richard L. Terrorism and guerrilla warfare. Routledge '90.

Connor, Michael. Terrorism. Paladin '87.

Der Derian, James. Antidiplomacy. Blackwell '92.

Dobson, Christopher; Payne, Ronald. The never-ending war. Facts on File '87.

Ehrenfeld, Rachel. Narco-terrorism. Basic '90.

Finn, John E. Constitutions in crisis. Oxford Univ. Press '91.

Gal-Or, Noemi. International cooperation to suppress terrorism. St. Martin's '85.

Gearty, Conor. Terror. Faber & Faber. '91.

Gilbert, Paul. Terrorism, security, and nationality. Routledge '94.

Grosscup, Beau. The explosion of terrorism. New Horizon '87.

Guelke, Adrian. The age of terrorism and the international political system. Tauris Studies '95.

Han, Henry Hyunwook. Terrorism & political violence. Oceana '93.

Hanle, Donald J. Terrorism. Pergamon-Brassey's '89.

Herman, Edward S.; O'Sullivan, Gerry. The terrorism industry. Pantheon '90.

Hewitt, Christopher. Consequences of political violence. Dartmouth '93.

Holms, John Pynchon; Burke, Tom. Terrorism. Windsor '94.

Hyland, Francis P. Armenian terrorism. Westview '91.

Kent Layne. A political organization approach to transnational terrorism. Greenwood '86.

Lambert, Joseph J. Terrorism and hostages in international law. Grotius '90.

Laqueur, Walter. The age of terrorism. Weidenfeld & Nicolson '87.

Leeman, Richard W. The rhetoric of terrorism and counterterrorism. Greenwood '91.

Lesce, Tony. Wide open to terrorism. Loompanics Unlimited '96.

Lightbody, Andy. The terrorism survival guide. Dell '87.

Livingstone, Neil C.; Arnold, Terrell E. Fighting back. Lexington '86.

Martin, John McCullough; Romano, Anne T. Multinational crime. Sage '92.

Melman, Yossi. The master terrorist. Adama '86.

Merkl, Peter H. Political violence and terror. University of Calif. Press '86.

Mulgrew, Ian. Unholy terror. Key Porter '88.

Netanyahu, Benjamin. Terrorism. Farrar, Straus & Giroux '86.

O'Kane, Rosemary H. T. The revolutionary reign of terror. Elgar '91.

Poland, James M. Understanding terrorism. Prentice-Hall '88.

Ra'anan, Uri. Hydra of carnage. Lexington '86.

Rapoport, David C. Inside terrorist organizations. Columbia Univ. Press '88.

Rapoport, David C.; Alexander, Yonah. The Morality of terrorism. Columbia Univ. Press '89.

Rivers, Gayle. The war against the terrorists. Stein & Day '86.

Schaffert, Richard W. Media coverage and political terrorists. Praeger '92.

Schlagheck, Donna M. International terrorism. Lexington '88.

Schlesinger, Philip. Media, state, and nation. Sage '91.

Scotti, Anthony J. Executive safety and international terrorism. Prentice-Hall '86.

Seale, Patrick. Abu Nidal; a gun for hire. Arrow '93.

Sederberg, Peter C. Terrorist myths. Prentice-Hall '89.

Segaller, Stephen. Invisible armies. Harcourt '87.

Slann, Martin W.; Schechterman, Bernard. Multidimensional terrorism. Rienner '87.

Sloan, Stephen. The pocket guide to safe travel. Contemporary '86.

St. John, Peter. Air piracy, airport security, and international terrorism. Quorum '91.

Stohl, Michael. The Politics of terrorism. Dekker '88.

Stohl, Michael; Lopez, George A. Government violence and repression. Greenwood '86.

Szumski, Bonnie. Terrorism. Greenhaven '86.

Taylor, Maxwell. The terrorist. Brassey's '88.

Taylor, Maxwell; Quayle, Ethel. Terrorist lives. Brassey's '94.

Trager, Oliver. Fighting terrorism. Facts on File '86.

Turner, Stephen. Terrorist explosive sourcebook. Paladin '94.

Vetter, Harold J.; Perlstein, Gary R. Perspectives on terrorism. Brooks/Cole '91.

Warner, Martin; Crisp, Roger. Terrorism, protest and power. Elgar '90.

Waugh, William L. Terrorism and emergency management. Dekker '90.

Weinberg, Leonard B.; Davis, Paul. Introduction to political terrorism. McGraw-Hill '89.

White, Jonathan Randall. Terrorism. Brooks/Cole '91.

Wieviorka, Michel. The making of terrorism. Univ. of Chicago '93.

Wilkinson, Paul. Terrorism and the liberal state. New York Univ. Press '86.

Wilkinson, Paul; Stewart, Alasdair M. Contemporary research on terrorism. Aberdeen Univ. Press '87.

Yallop, David A. To the ends of the earth; the hunt for the Jackal. Corgi '94.

Yallop, David A. Tracking the Jackal. Random '93.

Additional Periodical Articles with Abstracts

The chemistry of mass murder. Frederick V. Guterl. *Discover* 17:72 Ja '96

Part of a special issue on science in 1995. The bomb that exploded underneath a government building in Oklahoma City on April 19, killing 168 people, largely consisted of common fertilizer. When combined with a flammable material such as diesel fuel, common fertilizer based on ammonium nitrate can supply the oxygen required for the fuel to burn even when no air is present. Aluminum, zinc, or potassium sulfate must be added to the mixture to lower the temperature threshold above which the compound will explode. When all these materials are confined in a closed space with a detonator, the makings of a bomb are present. Following the Oklahoma City bombing, there have been calls to have fertilizer chemically treated so that it cannot be used for terrorist purposes, or to have chemical "markers" added to make it easier to trace.

A killer's essay. Rae Corelli. *Maclean's* 108:57 O 2 '95

The publication of a serial killer's manifesto last week with the support of two of North America's most influential and respected newspapers has triggered debate among journalists and academics. At the request of U.S. Attorney General Janet Reno and the FBI, *The Washington Post*, with the concurrence and financial support of *The New York Times*, published the 35,000-word manifesto of the so-called Unabomber, who has killed three people and injured 23 others in 16 mail bombings since 1978. The Unabomber promised not to kill again if his manifesto were published. Some journalists and academics agreed with *Times* publisher Arthur Sulzberger Jr. and *Post* publisher Donald Graham that given the further threat to human life, the two newspapers had no other choice. Other critics asserted that the decision was ethically and morally wrong because it compromised the newspapers' public trust and will encourage imitators. The article describes the manifesto.

Earth First! the press and the Unabomber. Alexander Cockburn. *The Nation* 262:9-10 My 6 '96

Within four days of the arrest of alleged Unabomber Theodore Kaczynski, the radical environmental group *Earth First!* was being accused by a TV network of fomenting murder. Within 48 hours of the arrest, ABC *World News Tonight* ran a lead story in which reporter Brian Ross conveyed the news that "authorities" believed Kaczynski was present at a November 1994 meeting in Montana attended by top members of Earth First!, a group under investigation by the FBI. Two days later, Ross, during an appearance on *This Week with David Brinkley*, left the heavy implication that the death of Thomas Mosser, one of the Unabomber's victims, had been plotted at the November meeting According to the organizers of the conference, however, no name even remotely resembling that of the alleged Unabomber has been found on the attendance rosters.

The Iraq papers. *The New Republic* 214:12 + Ja 29 '96

Despite the Pentagon's announcement of the demise of Iraq's nuclear and chemical weapons programs on January 21, 1991, new information shows how close a call it really was. It now appears from newly declassified U.S. intelligence reports and captured Iraqi documents that Saddam Hussein actually gave orders to his field commanders to use chemical weapons against Allied forces but that these were not obeyed. Also, the documents show that Iraq had filled its extended-range SCUD missiles and aerial bombs with biological warfare agents and used these on the battlefield. Gulf War veterans' groups believe that more than 70,000 vets and their dependents may be suffering as a result of low-level exposure to biological and chemical agents released into the atmosphere by these bombings. The most astonishing revelation contained in the new Pentagon documents may well be the extent of knowledge that was available to the U.S. intelligence community on Iraq's chemical and biological programs before the war.

Western showdown. *Newsweek* 125:39 Ap 17 '95

Discord between Westerners and the federal government has turned violent. Westerners resent federal administration of large areas of land in their region. Bomb explosions have rocked Forest Service and Bureau of Land Management offices in Nevada, and the agencies have started advising employees on ways to protect themselves from hostile locals. No one has yet been injured in such incidents, but that may happen soon.

A shadow over the Olympics. Tom Morganthau. *Newsweek* 127:34-5 My 6 '96

The federal authorities are preparing to counter threats to the Atlanta Olympics. The multibillion-dollar event, which will attract 2 million spectators, thousands of athletes, and 40 heads of state, is a security nightmare. There are a variety of disaffected groups nursing dangerous grudges: American right-wingers, religious sects, breakaway ethnic groups, and Arab fundamentalists. The U.S. militia movement, in particular, is now a plausible source of terrorism, and, because militia adherents organize themselves into tiny cells, they are very difficult to detect or infiltrate. Furthermore, there is a greater availability of once unobtainable means of destruction—bombs, chemical and biological agents, and even nuclear weapons. With the Olympics just three months away, federal authorities are constructing possibly the largest counterterrorist operation in history, involving the FBI, the CIA, the Secret Service, local and state police, and U.S. military units.

The Fed's quiet war. Daniel Klaidman and Michael Isikoff. *Newsweek* 127:47 Ap 22 '96

Domestic terrorism is rising to levels not seen since the late 1960s and early 1970s, when there was a rash of bombings by student radicals and militants. According to the Southern Poverty Law Center, there are 440 self-proclaimed antigovernment militias active in every U.S. state. Although the FBI says that many of the militiamen are little more than "Internet commandos," it takes the extremists seriously. At the Justice Department, for example, a secret task force called the Executive Working Group on Domestic Terrorism meets every two weeks, culls intelligence, and plans strategy. Since the group was set up last year, FBI investigations of militias have increased fourfold. Two recent bombings that may have been the work of the Aryan Republican Army are discussed.

Long-running Unabom case continues to perplex the F.B.I. *New York Times* A13 Ap 24 '95

(April 23) More than 20 agents from the Federal Bureau of Investigation, the Treasury Department, and the Postal Service have worked on the case code-named Unabom, whose central figure has set off 15 bombings in the last 17 years. According to Rick Smith of the San Francisco F.B.I. office, the bomber's motivation and demands are unknown.

Raiding a Vipers' nest. *New York Times* A18 Jl 4 '96

The infiltration, indictment, and disarmament of a disturbingly well-armed paramilitary cell called the Viper Militia may have spared Arizona and the nation another burst of home-grown terrorism. It is now clear that unknown militia groups can be plotting to blow up federal buildings—and that the government can find and stop them.

Agents seize arsenal of rifles and bomb-making material in Arizona militia inquiry.
New York Times A18 Jl 3 '96

July 2—Federal agents today seized more than 100 high-powered rifles and hundreds of pounds of a bomb-making compound from the Phoenix house of a man who officials said is the ordnance specialist of a local paramilitary group. On Monday the suspect, Gary C. Bauer, and 11 other people were arrested on charges of conspiring to blow up government buildings in Phoenix.

Prosecutor in bombings is called unflappable. John Sullivan. *New York Times* A20 Ap 12 '96

Colleagues and former opponents of Robert J. Cleary, the first assistant U.S. attorney in the Northern District of New Jersey and the man appointed to head the Unabom prosecution team, say that Cleary is smart, thorough, and calm, even when everyone else is panicking and a case is falling apart. This latter ability will be helpful in the expected prosecution of Theodore J. Kaczynski, suspected by the FBI of having conducted a bombing campaign for almost 18 years from a small cabin in the Montana wilderness.

Oklahoma City suspect wants secret documents. Jo Thomas. *New York Times* A12 Ap 10 '96

April 9—Stephen Jones, chief lawyer for Timothy J. McVeigh, told Judge Richard P. Matsch of Federal District Court today that he could not defend his client without access to classified documents of the Central Intelligence Agency, the Defense Intelligence Agency, and the National Security Agency. Jones said that he had evidence from a variety of sources that the bombing of the federal building in Oklahoma City last year had been financed and carried out by a foreign terrorist group, and he asked the judge to read a sealed motion stating why the defendants needed the documents.

Bomber inquiry shifts to tactics for legal case. Ralph Blumenthal. *New York Times* A1 + Ap 6 '96

April 5—As investigators hauled away what they said was a mountain of evidence linking Theodore J. Kaczynski to the Unabom attacks, authorities began building their case against the Montana recluse. Federal law enforcement officials voiced confidence that the explosives, notebooks, and other objects found in Kaczynski's cabin would tie the former math professor to mail bombings that left three people dead and 23 injured.

L.I. bomb threat closes La Guardia, J.F.K. and Newark. Robert D. McFadden. *New York Times* A1 + Ag 29 '95

A bomb threat that forced the evacuation of a critical air traffic control center on Long Island shut down the New York metropolitan area's three major airports for more than an hour yesterday, delaying hundreds of arrivals and departures and affecting hundreds of other plane movements in a ripple effect across the U.S. Yesterday's disruption added one more headache to the troubles of the Federal Aviation Administration, whose air traffic control system has been plagued all year by power failures, the loss of telephone communications, and glitches in an antiquated computer system.

House G.O.P. madness. Thomas L. Friedman. *New York Times* A15 Ap 3 '96

In the wake of the Oklahoma City and World Trade Center bombings, a bill strengthening the F.B.I.'s ability to fight terrorism would seem to be an obvious step. The fact that it is not suggests that the soul of the Republican Party, at least in the House of Representatives, is now dominated by lawmakers who despise their own government more than they fear foreign terrorists. The real work of gutting H.R. 2703, the comprehensive Anti-Terrorism Act, was done by the National Rifle Association and the gun lobby, which lobbied the Freshmen Republicans quite effectively.

The Oklahoma indictments. *New York Times* A20 Ag 12 '95

The striking thing about the indictments recently issued by a Federal grand jury in the Oklahoma City bombing case is the revelation of how small-time the operation behind the terrorist act may turn out to be. Prosecutors and the grand jury seem to have concluded that the bombing was primarily the work of two drifters who used ordinary, inexpensive materials to pack a rental truck with 4,800 pounds of homemade explosives. While it is reassuring to know that there may not be an organized conspiracy ready to carry out other terrorist bombings, it is disturbing to learn just how vulnerable American society is to the acts of a handful of crazed outcasts.

Monitoring the U.S. mail. Marc Saxon. *Popular Electronics* 13:72-3 Ap '96

Investigating criminal activity related to the mail service and enforcing law are the responsibility of the U.S. Postal Inspection Service. More than 2,000 agents are located across the country, and they perform surveillance, serve federal warrants and subpoenas, and make arrests. In addition, the postal service has an extensive armed, uniformed security force. These important enforcement and security activities have never been fully appreciated by scanner users, however. The writer reviews Radio Shack's triple-conversion PRO 60 scanner, lists frequencies for the U.S. Postal Service and for the FAA at some airports, discusses the controversial book *Tune In on Telephone Calls!*, and suggests frequencies to monitor the Eldorado National Forest in Placerville, California.

Research pays off. Vinton G. Cerf. *Science* 271:1343 Mr 8 '96

The Advanced Research Projects Agency (ARPA) has produced an abundance of technological breakthroughs that have greatly benefited U.S. national security. ARPA was formed in the late 1950s to help America avoid technological surprises, and it has furthered national security in militarily relevant results and through expansion of the country's technology base, upon which industry has drawn to produce new services, products, and businesses. The undertaking of ARPA to make its results readily shared and widely known has paid off in new product developments funded by industry and based on freely available research results, source software, prototypes, and the like. Many ARPA-sponsored research efforts have had 100 percent or more matching funding from industry, and companies not able to justify the risks alone can do so in conjunction with ARPA and in other industry consortia cooperating with the government.

Global positioning for all. Richard Monastersky. *Science News* 149:212 Ap 6 '96

According to a recent White House announcement, civilians are to be given access to the Global Positioning System (GPS) some time in the next ten years. U.S. military forces can locate their position to within eight meters instantly using the GPS, a constellation of 24 air force satellites circling the earth. The Department of Defense has been degrading the signal allowed to civilians, however, for reasons of national security. The decision to stop corrupting the GPS signal was taken in response to the increasing ability of commercial firms to improve the accuracy of the degraded GPS data to within a few meters, making security measures less effective. The Department of Defense plans to develop new ways of preventing enemy interception of GPS data. According to the Clinton administration, free worldwide access to GPS will stimulate an already fast growing commercial market for GPS equipment.

Playing with fire. Jack E. White. *Time* 147:44 Mr 18 '96

Over the past 18 months, while Republicans denounced welfare and affirmative action, more than 20 black churches in Alabama and six other Southern and border states have been burned down. Despite an investigation by federal and state authorities, it is still uncertain whether organized hate groups or lone lunatics are responsible for the fires. To the blacks who live there, however, the motive is clearly intimidation. Moreover, they are convinced the politicians who have stoked the fires of hatred should be held accountable for creating an atmosphere in which such terrorism is conceivable. Indeed, all the conservative Republicans who have sought political gain by exploiting white resentment should visit the charred ruins of the New Liberty Baptist Church in Tyler, a tiny hamlet ten miles east of Selma, Alabama, and consider if their coded phrases influenced the arsonists.

An armed fanatic raises the stakes. Michael D. Lemonick. *Time* 145:34-5 Ja 9 '95

Deadly attacks on two clinics in Brookline, Massachusetts, have raised a national outcry over unchecked antiabortion violence Police identified 22-year-old John C. Salvi III as the man who shot to death receptionists Shannon Lowney of Planned Parenthood and Leanne Nichols of Preterm Health Services. After his rampage, Salvi was allegedly involved in another nonfatal shooting at the Hillcrest Clinic in Norfolk, Virginia, where he was arrested shortly thereafter. The shootings brought to five the number of abortion-clinic killings nationwide in the last two years. Countless lesser acts of violence against abortion providers and their patients, including verbal and physical harassment, assaults, and firebombings, have also occurred. The federal government's response to antiabortion violence is discussed.

Of frights and flights. David Van Biema. *Time* 146:49 S 11 '95

Two major problems now burden the Federal Aviation Administration: terrorist fears and the physical disintegration of the FAA's massive and antique air-traffic infrastructure. The article discusses recent flight delays caused by worries about increased terrorist activity and a Fremont, California, blackout in mid-August that grounded hundreds of planes.

Where is John Doe no. 2? Brian Duffy. *U.S. News & World Report* 120:33 Ap 22 '96

The Oklahoma City bombing will prove a difficult case for the prosecution. Headed by Joseph Hartzler, the prosecution has indicted Timothy McVeigh and Terry Nichols for the bombing, which killed over 168 people, but the indictment also charges "others unknown" to the FBI. According to a senior law enforcement official, a vigorous search continues for "John Doe No. 2," whois suspected of accompanying McVeigh when he allegedly rented the truck that carried the bomb. Another problem for Hartzler will be his star witness, Michael Fortier, who is expected to testify that he surveyed the Alfred P. Murrah Federal Building in Oklahoma City as a potential bomb target with McVeigh four months before the bombing. Defense lawyers will cross-examine Fortier about his use of various illegal drugs in the period prior to the bombings and challenge his credibility by referring to the numerous media interviews that Fortier gave in which he denied that McVeigh was responsible for the bombing. Other prosecution problems include witness statements that are inconsistent on crucial points of timing and personal appearance.

Appendix A

Organizations Involved with Terrorism Analysis

The Heritage Foundation — (1973) Joseph Coors and New Right activist Paul Weyrich with Richard Mellon Scaife helped establish this affluent organization which has served a variety of institutions of the extreme right.

Georgetown Center for Strategic and International Studies (CSIS) — (1970s) Headed by David Abshire, CSIS places emphasis on terrorism research with many prestigious experts in the field of terrorism.

The RAND Corporation — (1948) A think tank for the U.S. Air Force, is a major source of independent, nonprofit research and education. RAND also studies national security problems in Central America.

The National Forum Foundation (NFF) — (1982) Organized in 1977 by Jeremiah Denton, was initially designed to educate the public on the nuclear freeze movement and made further breakthroughs in the Soviet network theory of terrorism.

The Jewish Institute for National Security Affairs (JINSA) — (Late 1970s) Run by many individuals closely identified with Israeli interests and a virtual lobbying organization for the state of Israel, as well as an institute for the study of terrorism.

Institute for Studies in International Terrorism, State University of New York (ISIT) — (1977) Yonah Alexander with the State University of New York (Oneonta) had extensive international ties to military, police, and intelligence operations. Chronologies of terrorist "acts" also provide anaylsis and examination of these studies.

United States Global Strategy Council (USGSC) — (1981) The aims of this organization are to promote "global strategic planning" and "to act as a catalyst to help define national strategy" along lines desired by its hard-right board. It sponsors outreach programs as well as research and conferences on various international issues.

The Nathan Hale Institute — (1977) They track and provide information on terrorist organizations and their supporters. Formed by Raymond Wannall, this group keeps files on domestic terrorist operations and organizations.

American Security Council (ASC) — (1955) Created by Sears, Roebuck and Company, they have been involved in providing funding and logistical support for many other people involved with terrorism.

Appendix B

World Wide Web Sites*

Terrorism - U.S.Information Service

United States Information Service. Terrorism. Welcome to the United States Information Service (USIS) Gateway to Information on Terrorism. The Gateway...
URL: http://www.usia.gov/topical/terror/terror.htm.

Clinton Administration Counter Terrorism Initiative

Clinton Administration Counter Terrorism Initiative. I. Actions Already Announced by the President. (1) Pass the Omnibus Counter-Terrorism Act of 1995....
URL: http://www.cdt.org/policy/terrorism/adm-anti-terror-otl.html

Hearings on Wiretapping and other Terrorism Proposals

Hearings on Wiretapping and other Terrorism Proposals. Testimony of David B. Kopel Associate Policy Analyst Cato Institute. Committee on on the Judiciary..
URL: http://www.cato.org/testimony/ct5-24-5.html

Terrorism Context

Terrorism In The United States. The FBI defines terrorism as: "...the unlawful use of force or violence against persons or property to intimidate or...
URL: http://media.dickinson.edu/Clarke_Center/docs/terrorism_context.html

Controversial Anti-Terrorism Measure Signed into Law by Clinton

UNITED STATES. Controversial Anti-Terrorism Measure Signed into Law by Clinton. by Jeffrey Builta. With victims and families of victims of the World Trade.
—http://www.acsp.uic.edu/OICJ/PUBS/CJA/090317.htm

Local Terrorism Planning Model

Local Terrorism Planning Model. For most law enforcement agency administrators in the United States, the perceived threat of a terrorist act or attack...
URL: http://www.emergency.com/terrplan.htm

* All sites are subject to change.

Index